the art of
flower arrangement

the art of
flower arrangement

joyce rogers

hamlyn
london · new york · sydney · toronto

First Published in 1975 by
The Hamlyn Publishing Group Limited
London · New York · Sydney · Toronto
Astronaut House, Feltham, Middlesex, England
Filmset in Great Britain by Filmtype Services Limited
Printed and Bound in Czechoslovakia by Polygrafia, Prague

Acknowledgements
With gratitude I pay tribute to Theo Naude of
J.M.T. Studios, Cape Town, South Africa, my most efficient
and painstaking photographer. Flowers and children in
that order are the most difficult subjects to photograph,
requiring an abundance of skill and patience.
Thank you, Theo.

Dedication
In thankfulness to God our Father who has provided
so much beauty for our delight and
blessed us all with various talents, in the
use of which we realise a sense of fulfilment:
His peace and joy.

contents

displaying
the
flowers

Before you walk around the garden, or shop at the florist in search of flowers to arrange, you should use your imagination in a practical manner. First, site your arrangement. It is no good planning something which is going to get in the way either in the course of day-to-day living or on a special occasion. Remember that one sizeable design, in keeping with the dimensions of the room, will receive more attention than many little arrangements placed fussily here and there. The requirements of the household must be considered. You should avoid appropriating working space for flowers such as occasional tables which, as their name implies, are required for use maybe once or twice a day with consequent shuffling around of flowers and dumping of trays. Ideally there should be flower settings kept for that specific purpose and on the following pages you will find some helpful suggestions.

The needs of the flowers must also be met. A draughtless position, not too near any source of heat and out of direct sunshine, is their simple basic requirement. If the atmosphere is close and hot, give them plenty of space within their own confines and lots to drink. Open arrangements in shallow containers, with an expanse of water kept at a constant level, allow for free circulation of air around the base of the stems. These are cool to view as well as assuaging the thirst of the flowers. For extra thirsty subjects use deeper but still fairly wide-mouthed containers.

Green is a wonderful colour. An arrangement can be designed entirely around it using all the subtle shades, tints and tones. Green is very cooling in hot weather and it will soothe frayed nerves – an oasis of quiet calm to come home to. There are even green flowers which you can introduce such as arum lilies and gladioli and then there are the succulents fashioned as flowers like echeveria.

Foliage must be given a due place of honour because it is beautiful in its own right. It is invaluable when arranging and is economically a sound proposition. Although normally thought of as dreary, it is far from being that growing in many forms and with a great variation of colour. There is the silver and gold of elaeagnus, golden cupressus and golden privet, rich mahogany-red *Berberis thunbergii atropurpurea* and the beautiful, fiery-orange *Mahonia bealei*. Then there is also the less striking but always useful annual atriplex, ornamental kale and kitchen garden beetroot leaves to mention only a few. The soft silver greys of *Senecio greyii* and stachys present a further choice together with the ever-available help from colourful succulents and pot plants like tall caladium leaves and the smaller, but so satisfyingly colourful, rex begonias – an infinite variety to whet the appetite.

Flowers in the house – not necessarily a big or very grand house but anywhere appreciative people live – should complete the image of home, a place of happy togetherness busy with comings and goings where well-arranged fresh flowers or an artistic foliage arrangement will always provide a *pièce de résistance*.

If your style of interior decoration gives a busy impression – you may possess lots of lovely pictures which leave little clear wall space or you may own period furniture and ornaments which claim attention, or you may favour patterned wallpaper – then your floral designs must be able to stand out on their own. They must be, of necessity, a mass or semi-mass of materials and should be held in containers to harmonise with the surrounding *objets d'art*. This is where urns, Chinese vessels and stands, French and Victorian china come into their own.

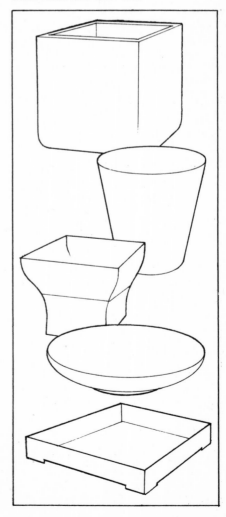

Massed display knocks back a busy background

Sweet peas are very suitable for arranging *en masse* because they have so little individuality of shape, depending for effect upon colour harmony and scent. Quite correctly, one always thinks of a huge bowl of sweet peas which, if they are sufficiently massed, can hold their own against all odds. I have used them to illustrate the fact that a mass or semi-mass design, which relies solely on colour outline, can be very effective against a busy background.

This fan-shaped arrangement in mauves and pinks stands in front of an ornate carved Chinese wall panel. The stems are contained in a gilded well-type pinholder

with a spray of rose buds and three lovely ranunculus in varying tints and tones of deep pink to provide more definition at the centre. It must be remembered that a mass of beautiful colours, when seen in their full glory, provides a separation between flowers and background which a black and white photograph is unable to convey.

You will notice that I have used no foliage. It is often better to dispense with this or keep it to a minimum in certain types of mass design. This is especially so when arranging sweet peas though a few of their own slender tendrils may be permitted. The use of foliage tends to reduce the strong visual appeal of these delicate flowers.

This arrangement could be one of the few instances where asparagus fern, *Asparagus sprengeri*, so beloved by florists and normally such a headache to the arranger, can be employed gainfully. Usually it is too light and feathery to satisfactorily accompany arranged flowers.

Line designs
are challenging and
aesthetic

If your taste is for a more contemporary or even very modern home, with comparatively unadorned walls decorated in quiet receding colours which demand less attention, then clever line designs, with greater character than the aforementioned lush arrangements, come into their own. These rely on quieter surroundings, without too much competition, to set them off to advantage.

This is a pure line design purposely set against a plain panelled wall using sweet peas again to show that they can occasionally be arranged in this way. However, lots of thought must go into such an arrangement as you will discover in the chapter on design. The mainspring of this composition was the accessory, the little old Chinaman, normally a bookend, who at home is affectionately known as John.

While I was looking around for something with which to create an unusual arrangement, my eye fell on John. My decision to employ him posed the problem of what to use for the container. I had the brainwave of cutting some bamboo from a grove in my garden into different lengths. The base of each pipe is formed by a natural joint or nodule. Used in this manner, as a series of containers, the bamboo holds water well and in sufficient quantity to maintain the few flower stems allotted to each 'pipe'. The five pieces, held together with a contact cement, were placed on a bamboo tray which welded all the components into a harmonious whole. The horizontal line of the tray is carried on by the base of the Chinese figure and the upright line of the bamboo-pipe container is reflected by the upright arrangement of the sweet peas, a line originated by the pipe played by John.

This is an ideal composition for a musical 'At Home' and it is a very easily executed arrangement, using only fifteen stems of sweet peas, once you have acquired the initial related parts. Bamboo is universally grown but cornstalks (corn-on-the-cob) make a good alternative.

Voids are as
important as flowers

Although this is not a stark line arrangement, there is nevertheless a good deal of free space or voids. These serve to emphasise the comparatively few flowers which is, of course, the essence of this type of arranging. Line arrangements can always be made to look different and interesting and there are many ways by which this can be achieved, as you will see in the pages of this book.

The magnolia branch, with its topmost buds just bursting into flower, is purposely carried up rather high in the design in order to counterbalance the depth of the double container. The unusual container is the distinguishing feature in this arrangement. Two identical heavy oblongs have been used with the second pivoted at an angle over the first. The smooth water-washed pebbles step the viewer's eye into the arrangement itself.

Two-into-one

People are very prone to standing arrangements of flowers upon windowsills. So long as their longevity is assured by not subjecting them to direct sunshine by day and sandwiching them between drawn curtains and cold glass at night, flowers in the window are a happy touch of welcome to home-coming family and visitors alike.

To be really effective you must create two arrangements within the one container. They must be identical in shape but can be unlike in colouring and choice of flowers. This gives you the chance of changing the arrangement around so that one day one side is viewed by passers-by; the next, that side is seen from within the house while the reverse side is presented to the outside.

The essential requirement is that the two arrangements are separated by a 'Pennine Range' of foliage. This backbone, through the centre width of the design, is made up of large-leaved foliage to form a background against which both sets of flowers in this dual arrangement will be seen at their best. It also serves to screen out excessive daylight and, in this way, throws into strong relief the arrangement facing into the room.

Aspidistra leaves are excellent for this purpose because they have a pleasing substance, are broadish with tapering height and, in addition, fall into graceful twists and turns which prevent a stiff strait-jacket appearance. Alternatives for smaller arrangements include hosta leaves, especially the variegated types, and the small leaves of arum lilies. The backbone could also be fashioned by the alternate use of solid, rounded leaves and taller, pointed foliage. For example *Bergenia saxifraga* or the less solid and prettily fluted leaves of statice could be arranged at the base with any blade-like foliage forming the upper outline.

The first picture was photographed in front of a mirror to reveal both sides of the two-sectional arrangement. The backbone is shown in position with the first five tulips of one side of the arrangement and the arums of the other. Although the arum design could simply have been neatened to finish it, I did add two semi-open smaller flowers for height, ensuring that they were each placed directly in front of a leaf and were therefore unable to be seen from the other side of the arrangement. It is imperative that neither of these two designs within one arrangement should intrude upon the other. Canna leaves are also to be seen

on the tulip side and arum leaves on the other. In the very plain, wide and oblong container, I used a heavy lead pinholder, held firmly in position by Oasis-fix in conjunction with 1½-in. mesh wire netting clearly shown here. The crumpled cut ends were uppermost as these are most useful for twisting around stems to give extra support to any difficult material.

The second picture shows the tulip arrangement completed with the addition of more tulips, kniphofia, iris and mimosa – a study in tawny orange and yellow. The reverse could consist of yellow or white flowers to keep the double arrangement in complete colour harmony when viewed by anyone leaning against the window. If preferred, the two arrangements could be identical in every way but why not take advantage of two facets of one gem – quite

a recommendation when materials are scarce and a quantity of any one thing is impossible to obtain.

The third picture is a modified side view to show the arranging technique. The arrangement would only be seen in this way by someone leaning against the window inside the room. For photographic purposes the further arum and accompanying leaf were lifted for this picture, to enable them to be seen clearly by the camera.

In the finished arrangement both leaves in fact lie almost horizontal with the container as depicted in the earlier reflected-in-the-mirror picture. A further two arums in graded stages of bud formation supplied the necessary height and completed this as yet unfinished arrangement.

A light
in the window

This arrangement of geraniums would be suitable for placing in the single window found beside the front door in many houses. It is a semi-line design in contrast to the mass two-in-one just shown. The rounded flower heads look equally good from both inside and outside the house and there are two further well-formed heads at the back of the base flowers which serve to complete the interior view of the arrangement.

There are many household objects, apart from traditional vases and containers, which lend themselves to flower arrangements when not occupied about their legitimate purposes. This wine-bottle holder is a souvenir from an Austrian holiday and it has given me inspiration for many new floral creations. On this occasion I have used it primarily as a candle holder. A non-drip, long-lasting candle, shaped and coloured to represent a flame, fits neatly into the socket normally occupied by the wine bottle. Instead of the goblet, which stands on the base below the bottle, a well pinholder has been used to contain the flame-coloured geraniums which combine with the black wrought-iron container to make a gay show.

At night, with the curtains undrawn, subdued hall lighting and the candle-light combine to give another most inviting welcome to hearth and home.

Window versus wall

The designers of modern houses and blocks of flats are keen on floor to ceiling windows. These are very pleasing in many ways but they do present problems when siting an arrangement. Wall space, without interrupting doors, is limited and is, in any case, keenly contested by furniture. I therefore seized the opportunity to use a space between two windows which is too narrow for a respectable piece of furniture but is just the place for a flower arrangement designed to fit. The curtains frame this tall narrow composition executed in bold materials.

A strong design is necessary for this position because a dainty one would call for a delicate container, and the setting of strong drapes and subdued in-between window lighting would overpower the arrangement. Leathery evergreen foliage is one of the greatest assets in the modern home where one needs arrangements of strong lines. I always rely on foliage because its clean-cut definition of form is always an inspiration. When very large leaves, like these palms, are used as the accent placement, they cannot be successfully supplanted by flowers but when used together they serve to dramatise the flowers.

Other accent or 'weight' foliage includes fig, aralia with its deep cut furrows, and monstera leaves with their striking irregular lobes. All are indispensable to any southern hemisphere garden along with vertical placement leaves such as the blade-like sansevieria and the colourful dracaenas. Classical acanthus, bold rhubarb foliage, ornamental kale and the superb *Mahonia bealei* are all equally at home in the northern hemisphere. Silvery-grey artichoke leaves are especially useful for curving lines and yucca, plain and variegated phormium and pampas grass should be grown in any arranger's garden – weather permitting. All these and many others can establish good line if used with precise placement. They are a boon to the modern arranger because of their long durability and less need for topping up because foliage gets by on less water than flowers.

The cotton palms, preserved to their delightful soft smokey-brown colour by immediate immersion of the cut stem ends in a solution of equal parts glycerine and water for about two weeks, are combined with brown spikes of wild seed heads to give a rich harmonious blending of muted browns and blue-greens.

The twisting stems are echoed in the movement of the swimming dragon on the metal Chinese vase while the touch of blue-green foliage between the palms makes an attractive link with the blue-green colouring of the container which stands on a simple brown oak stool.

To preserve foliage use one part glycerine to one part water in a one-pound jam jar or tin. Place a pinholder within to secure the stems, which must be fresh cut. These should not be given a previous drink of water. Peel and hammer one inch of the base of each woody stem and impale on the pins in at least four inches of the solution.

Leave for a fortnight or so to colour. Check that they are absorbing the fluid by touching the leaf tips. If these feel soft and silky within the first twenty-four hours and not dry and papery, they are absorbing the fluid and more water can be added to the solution as required. The plants will drink a substantial amount during the first few hours so watch the level of the solution carefully.

Suitable subjects for this treatment are palm and eucalyptus which turn smokey brown and mauve-grey respectively; beech, oak and Spanish chestnut which become golden; laurustinus, iris, juniper, yucca, pittosporum and magnolia which turn a variety of browns and *Azara microphylla* with a result resembling black lace. This last is a dainty compound leaf. It is most useful when preserved and arranged with delicate flowers.

Special effects

Built-in backgrounds

For special effects, drapes and built-in backgrounds can be brought into play as in the following colour plates.

The first, utilising sea plumes of delicate coral and lilies, is a good example of what I mean. The irregular incuts of the sea plumes are copied by nature in the indentations of the tubular lily flowers and my choice of the philodendron leaf gives another link in nature's wonderously varied yet similar pattern of growth.

The upper plume is held against the inside edge of a bronze-coloured well pinholder. It is secured by some Oasis-fix and is tall enough to provide the height needed for the low grouping of flowers. A smaller plume acts as the base on which the lilies appear to be placed, and this slopes gracefully upwards to the top front edge of the well pinholder where it is secured like its taller relative. The flower stems and the philodendron leaf are firmly impaled on the needles of the container within water.

By careful placement, the sea plumes form the impression of a natural casket opening to reveal a treasure. Short cut terminal elusters of the beautiful regal lily are used just as they grew and placed so as to follow the line of the casket. The lowest grouping is of three on one stem, the central grouping two on a stem with a further two on a stem comprising the top grouping.

When buying lilies of whatever type, endeavour to choose your stems according to the number of flower heads and in general opt for those carrying only two or three flowers. These cost less and avoid the heartbreak of discarding the extra flowers which invariably point the wrong way for the design of the arrangement. However, rejected flowers need not be wasted. In this arrangement the central head, just above the leaf, could easily have been a discarded singleton. The odd lily floret will also make a welcome decoration for a small desk accompanied by some suitable foliage such as a colourful rex begonia leaf, or a strap-shaped leaf to resemble the lily foliage, or a 'bodyguard' of garden iris foliage. Try it and see how good it looks.

If the lilies are home grown, remove the pollen from the stamens gently and carefully immediately on cutting, otherwise it spills, staining the purity of the flower and anything else with which it comes into contact. Florist-bought lilies have this operation performed by the grower before marketing but the buds will have to be de-pollinated as they open.

Drapes are usually associated with show work but they can be very attractive as backgrounds for home arrangements too. Just as an attractive square around the neck adorns us, so you can use a drape for flowers. A length of plain material is to be preferred but a patterned design can be used provided that the pattern is cleverly geared to the flowers. Drapes make a more impressive showing with very few floral materials. They can also provide another way of knocking back a fussy background.

I have several lengths of inexpensive tulle and also some chiffon. One piece of chiffon has broad pastel stripes of lime-green, yellow and apricot with each colour fading very gradually into its neighbour. This is wonderful because with it I can harmonise colour schemes. When using dahlias, for example, in their pale yellow and apricot tints, the chiffon is draped so that the yellow flowers show up against the apricot material and the apricot flowers gain strength from their softer yellow background. If I use the material as a base as well, I can manipulate it so that it contrasts with the colour of the container or matches it. There are endless variations which are all so easy to fix.

Practically invisible picture hooks can be used to hold up drapes. If, however, the location is on a good or highly polished piece of furniture into which it is impracticable to stick even the fine pin of a picture hook, a piece of Sellotape will do the trick, especially in combination with bouncy tulle which almost holds itself up provided you are generous with it.

The arrangement of anthuriums (page 21) was created for a corner. The drape was held in position by a picture hook which was concealed by the drape itself. The gleaming copper tray looks positively 'in the pink' as it reflects the colour of its surroundings.

The depth of green in the croton leaves is centred in the axils to form a striking background for the largest anthurium. The colour graduates via the leaf ribs and veins to the palest tints and tones of pink which lead the eye to the beauty of the flowers. The five anthuriums require nothing else. They decorate their corner with economical dash and fervour. Any extra flowers would immediately detract from this original effect.

The container used for the arrangement on this page was made by securing together two pieces of wood, both with an

interesting grain. The top one was set into a groove cut into the base piece to form a wooden casket from which golden daffodils and a few of their leaves spring out. The wood was thoroughly cleaned, scraped and then lightly varnished, a treatment which renders it more sophisticated as befits the way it is intended to use it.

The two substantial pieces are held firmly together by cabinet maker's glue. If less heavy wood had been used for the top,

then the deep slot in the base piece would have been sufficient to hold it. If this were the case, then the casket could be dismantled after use and the base employed in another arrangement.

An interesting stone, set at a gradient to follow the top line of the casket, fills the foreground with interest and conceals the small bowl of water in which the pinholder is surmounted by a small square of crumpled 1½-in. mesh wire netting through which the stems are inserted to provide additional security.

The members of the narcissus family need this extra assistance to hold their stems when they are arranged. Alternatively you can dispense with the wire netting and instead bind the extreme ends of their stems with a few twists of fuse wire. Otherwise the stems split and reflex back on themselves within a few hours and without one of these alternatives being practised they will lose their grip on the pinholder and not hold their position for long. If they are arranged in a deep container where crumpled wire netting supports them irrespective of a pinholder, then one can save the few minutes spent to bind the stem ends. On the whole, however, this family prefer shallow water to deep.

Wall niches

If more thought were given to the final decoration and furnishing of a house or flat, those responsible for designing the building would incorporate ideas which could result in many utilitarian and artistic improvements.

Moorish-type houses have the edge over the average type of house insomuch as they incorporate attractive and different-sized built-in niches originally intended for lamps, statuettes and other ornaments. Floral arrangements designed to fit these alcoves look stunning and are out of draughts and harm's way. If any of you reading this book are contemplating building a house, do insist on a niche or two. They can be built in to suit any type of house.

The vaulted church-type alcove is traditionally found in the moorish house. There is also the angular nook or any other variation of a cube that one can envisage for the modern home. If you think carefully about the siting of these niches, especially in regard to their relationship with the fireplace, doorways and windows, you will be richly rewarded.

All sorts of possibilities come to mind. Two nooks of equal size but at different heights on a short wall could house matching or contrasting pairs of arrangements. Another niche or a pair could lend interest to a fireplace surround.

If these are designed and incorporated at the time of building the house, one or two, or all if liked, can be wired for lighting effects. A bulb fitment beneath a false floor of heat-resistant glass gives a charming effect with diffused lighting rising from beneath the flowers. Enough space should be left under the false floor to allow for a free circulation of air around the bulb which will prolong its life. A sliding glass shelf is the most practicable since it will be easier to clean and also to replace the bulb.

If you wish to adapt this idea to an existing house, you can build a hanging cupboard a foot or so above standing-eye level to form a frame in which to display an ever-varying floral picture. Introduce concealed lighting, and colourwash it to fade unobtrusively into the wall or you can boldly feature it by incorporating a picture frame. An ornate surround would be suitable for a period home or something simple for a modern home. You may have a window which is not really necessary and this, too, can be turned into the most attractive niche.

Planter room divider

While on the subject of building, do seriously consider a built-in plant trough at floor level. This could act as a room divider or it could be an extension of the window-sill, from sill to floor. This latter position is particularly favourable with regard to light for pot plants, especially those with colourful foliage if they are to achieve and maintain full colour. It is also easier with this position to arrange for water seepage or drainage by building in weep holes on the external wall. These will help in keeping the planter adequately watered and also overcome the usual pitfall of over-watered planters. They can so easily become waterlogged with a resulting loss of aeration, onset of fungus and other such troubles terminating in the end of healthy plants. I would even go so far as to make a plea that when the house design is planned that a room-divider planter is plumbed in as part of the general plumbing.

Another practical help to the plants and to the owners of centrally heated homes is to incorporate a 'pool' to provide humidity. These can either be on a big scale for large houses and public offices or a mere 24-in. long, 3-in. deep by 9-in. wide affair. They will keep the room humidity at a constant level for the better enjoyment and health of both plants and humans, and if the planting is landscaped down to the edge of the pool, it will turn necessity into eye-catching virtue. They can be made to look still more natural by incorporating interesting bits of rocks, pebbles, shells, coral or anything else that takes your fancy and which will be in keeping and improve the general appearance.

In this manner, even in the northern hemisphere, many attractive and useful house plants can be easily grown, given adequate light and humidity for their type requirements. Maximum available light is needed for coloured and variegated foliage and for flowering plants; less light sufficing for the obliging monstera and fatshedera, for example. The foliage begonia varieties – flower arrangers' delights – are exceptions to the rule that colourful leaves require light. They love a darker spot, within reason of course. If you bear in mind that they are grown commercially in a well-shaded glasshouse, this will help you to house them comfortably. Sansevierias are easy subjects either in full light or away from it. Bromeliads, whose flowers last for a couple of months, give much pleasure indoors. Different species ensure a succession of flowers from February till late October. Most of the foliage used in this book can easily be grown by the reader in this way. Leaves can be cut as required, remembering that you never need many and once cut they last a very long time in arrangements.

How about separating the shower from the rest of the bathroom with a trough of plants? There is nothing like sharing a bath with Mother-in-law's tongue but do allow plenty of room for the human species. I found it tough going fighting for bath space in our son-in-law's home. Our daughter loves plants, but slipping on the soap and sitting on a cactus is not exactly as happy as it sounds!

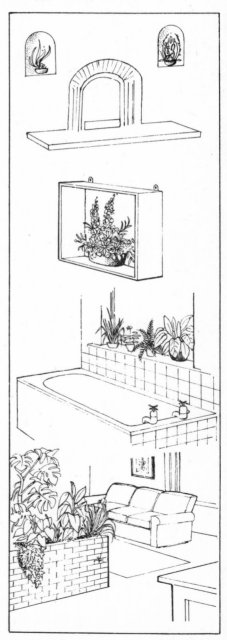

Containers

The word container covers a multitude of unlike shapes which have one all-important basic essential in common. They must be able to contain water in sufficiency for any given arrangement of flowers and foliage. Some flowers like the bulbous iris, tulip and daffodil and blade-like foliage such as phormium, iris, aspidistra and sansevieria require a minimum and are happily and effectively displayed in shallow dishes.

Annuals, perennials and most shrubs usually require deeper containers so that their stems can be submerged in at least three to four inches, maybe more. Roses appreciate deep water and anemones are notoriously thirsty subjects. However, because the latter grow on fairly short stems, they have to be displayed in small bowls and shallow containers so a special topping-up service must be resorted to.

This simple arrangement is held in a milk jug with a little wire netting to keep the stems in place. It is wise to cut anemone stems under water before arranging them. Most fleshy stems will benefit from this extra trouble to offset air blockages to which they are prone. Metalware and wood containers have a certain superiority over ceramics and glass because they 'breathe' and this keeps the water sweet and prolongs the life of the materials.

Aesthetically glass is least attractive because it reveals a confusion of stem ends which detract from the finished arrangement. One way to surmount this difficulty is to line the insides of glass goblets and wine glasses with evergreen foliage. I stress evergreen as deciduous foliage does not look so good and soon becomes smelly. The smooth grey leaves of the dainty senecios are very attractive as they give a silver-opaque patterned effect to the glass, reminiscent of Swedish glassware. They remain free of algae and last a long time.

How to secure stems in the container

There are three main ways to secure the stems so that everything stays put the way you intend.

Pinholders or needle points, as they are sometimes called, are heavy bases of lead studded with very sharp short brass pins.

The closer packed, shorter, and heavier they are, the better they will hold the stems, and I prefer those without rubber suction bases.

Pinholders are available in different sizes and can be the more usual round shape, oblong or even square. The authentic Japanese kenzans are perfect in every way, heavy, short, close-set, with non-rust, very sharp pins (needles) and some are designed to lock into one another to make a bigger unit as the arrangement requires. When used separately, the relative convex and corresponding concave areas fit so neatly into the round curves of a bowl.

For big arrangements, in which light driftwood and heavy woody stems are used such as branches of foliage or shrub stems like lilac, philadelphus (mock orange) or forsythia, a much bigger pinholder is designed and this one has its pins set slightly further apart to allow for these thick stems. Even so you must cut each stem end into a point, much as you would sharpen a thick pencil. If you do not practise this way of cutting this particular type of stem when using it in a pinholder, not only will the pinholder suffer damage but the stems will not be secure. These pinholders, however, are not so useful for general arranging and one or two should suffice the average requirements for home arrangements.

People often query how to fix the bigger pieces of driftwood they acquire. Individual pieces require separate treatment but if they are light enough and cut correctly, it is sometimes possible to impale them along with the flowers in shallow containers. Medium-heavy pieces that substitute for actual flowers or foliage stems may sometimes require the additional help of a wadge of Plasticine or preferably a suitable contact cement to help keep their place. Deep containers present no problems with correct and sufficient wiring. Heavier wood, if it is to be used as part of the base or an accessory, must be grooved and chiselled to provide a point of firm self-supporting balance.

I find the well pinholder most useful and treasure mine. It is invaluable for use with unorthodox containers and for more original arrangements featuring driftwood, which I unashamedly adore, use and defend, because the line is the thing and driftwood has it, every time.

If you are unable to purchase a well pinholder, then fashion yourself one with a suitable-sized tin. I often use one of those gilt-painted tins in which sweets are sold at chemists. I varnish the inside to prevent rust, fit it with a 3-in. diameter pinholder and I am away. I have also made my own with soft lead in the shape of an oblong and fitted it with an oblong pinholder for narrow spots in the crevices of wood. The manufactured ones are best of course because they are flowerpot shaped and fit into tight spots much better.

Whatever you use, remember always to keep the pins well awash with water and your flowers will not go thirsty.

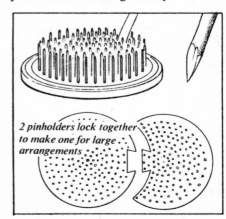

2 pinholders lock together to make one for large arrangements

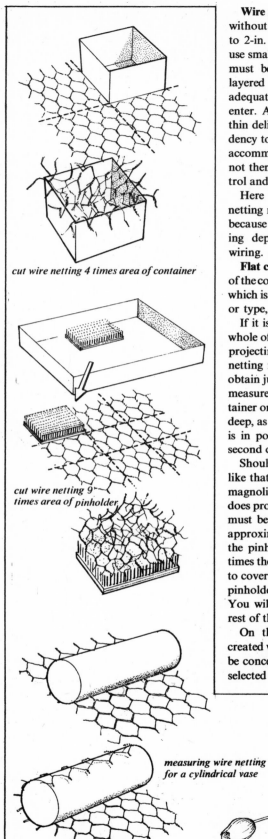

cut wire netting 4 times area of container

cut wire netting 9 times area of pinholder

Wire netting is a great aid used with or without a pinholder. Soft, rustproof 1½- to 2-in. fine-gauge mesh is best. Do not use smaller mesh because to be effective it must be lightly crumpled into a many layered mound and yet there must be adequate-sized holes for the stems to enter. A fine mesh restricts you to very thin delicate stems with the resultant tendency to crumple the wire less in order to accommodate the bigger stems. There is not then sufficient depth of twists to control and prevent stem movement.

Here are ideas of the amount of wire netting required per type of arrangement because so much of the success of arranging depends on correct and adequate wiring.

Flat containers Regardless of the shape of the container, the amount of wire netting which is needed corresponds to the design, or type, of the flower arrangement.

If it is to be a mass design utilising the whole of the container with no part of this projecting clear of the flowers, then the netting must fill the entire container. To obtain just the right amount cut a piece to measure four times the area of the container or more if the container is relatively deep, as shown here in the line drawing. It is in position for mass arranging in the second drawing.

Should you be wanting a line design, like that for example of tulips, iris, and a magnolia branch in which the container does project (page 9) then the wire netting must be cut to a square which measures approximately three times the diameter of the pinholder to be wired or about nine times the area. It should then be crumpled to cover only the immediate area over the pinholder as shown in the line drawings. You will note how relatively clear is the rest of the container.

On the whole, line designs are best created with pinholders only which should be concealed by the use of various things selected for their suitability and contribu-

tion to the overall design. Moss can be used for a natural-looking driftwood and narcissi arrangement; stones or pebbles for a water design, and washed coal for a real mod.

Cylindrical vases – deep containers – are measured by wrapping netting, which measures the depth of the container, once round it rather like the proverbial 'once around your fist for your correct stocking size'. Press the netting into the vase with a slight corkscrew-like twist, keeping the cut ends uppermost.

Always crumple the wire with these cut ends, or outside edges, facing upwards. Then you will always have a number of ends available to help deal with recalcitrant stems. It is always an advantage to twist one such cut end of wire around the base of the first stem, which is usually the most important and the longest in the composition, thus giving it extra support.

Another valuable use for these cut ends is to press them down gently upon a curved stem so that they hold it and prevent it from straightening, as some are prone to do when put in water. The gentle pressure will not hurt the flowers and will keep them firmly in place. This is a great asset when dealing with such flowers as tulips or anemones which so love to re-arrange themselves! Wire netting ends also help to hold firm horizontal or severely angled stems which cannot be impaled on the pinholder.

Cellular bricks, plastic foam, work on the osmotic system and are very useful for certain types of containers such as figurines, shells or other ornaments which may possess an area which will hold water but are not suitable for a pinholder and wire netting either because they are uneven or are too dainty.

Cellular bricks are ideal for use with silver and plate articles to avoid scratching and staining and it is the only medium for extremely shallow holders like, for instance, an ashtray which could not con-

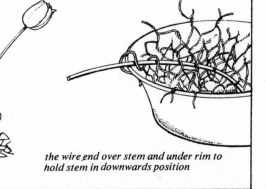

measuring wire netting for a cylindrical vase

twists of wire netting for additional support where necessary

the wire end over stem and under rim to hold stem in downwards position

cellular brick

candlecup

candlestick or figurine

Convert your precious pieces

This pastel-tinted fine china figurine is often brought down from the shelf – of honour, I must add. It lends itself to many dainty arrangements utilising the smaller flowers like these palest pink marguerites.

The decorative holes below the scalloped rim can be made watertight by the use of minute pieces of Bostik pres-stik or Oasis-fix, both harmless contact cements. The former is white in colour, the latter green. These substances are of great assistance in many spheres, as the instructions inform you. I find this material invaluable for holding things together especially pinholders within containers.

Here minute pieces are inserted into the holes. It is essential that the Bostik, one's hands and the container are all perfectly dry when positioning, after which it is impervious to water which can now be poured in up to the rim, if necessary. Easily removable, it is a great asset when using precious items as temporary flower holders and is especially useful when silver is in service because no marks are left. I prefer to use this material with this figurine to avoid any chance of damage to this special container.

Select either an oblong or round block of the cellular brick of your choice and cut a piece using a sharp knife to conform as close as possible to the shape of the water container you are using. It must be one unbroken piece, so cut it accurately before its preliminary soak.

The waterholding 'cup' of this container is a tapering oval in shape and so the inevitable gap between the oval and a round or square block of cellular brick allows a little space for easier topping-up. The great thing is to ensure a really firm fit like a size six foot in a size five-and-a-half shoe! After soaking, place it over the container and with the palm of the hand gently but firmly press it home.

If the shape of the block is perfect, for example a square within a square, which leaves no water-filling space, just top-up over the surface area. If you remember to keep the brick thoroughly damp all the time everything will be fine.

When using this type of stem holder you must be fairly sure of your stem placement. You cannot keep changing your mind. If you do, a morass of crumbling holes will make things difficult for you.

It is an ideal material for use with designs requiring emphasised curves, which may not be natural to the plant, because the stems can reach their water supply almost upside down.

Firm slender stems are best suited to this type of material. Sappy stems have to follow a lead given them by prior insertion of a fine knitting needle and they do not last so well.

tain a sufficient depth of water to cover a pinholder completely and would therefore be useless as a container if these 'bricks' were not available.

Once the plastic sponge-like material is thoroughly pre-soaked in a basin for about half an hour or until it sinks, all that is required is to keep it moist. Half-an-inch of water in the base of a shallow container is sufficient if it is kept replenished. So long as it is thoroughly wet all the time it is in use, the floral materials will last well. Details of the use of the above are given where necessary throughout the book.

Pinholders and wire netting can be combined in large mass arrangements while line designs are better with pinholders alone, but always ensure that these foundations are firm and sufficient for the requirements of your design. They are as important to the arrangement as braces and suspenders to trousers and stockings!

proportion – the first and basic essential

The various parts of an arrangement are interrelated both to one another and to the whole in height, width and depth. Proportion and form are largely responsible for the general effect with beauty and clarity of line resulting from our artistic instincts working in conjunction with certain mathematical rules.

The Greeks worked with material from natural sources such as rock and clay and they imparted order and balance where previously there was none. This urge to improve upon nature was deployed in large sculptures as well as in humbler arts like decorations on pottery and in their depiction of floral motives. They always, however, used restraint in the process as must the flower arranger when handling the raw materials of this particular art form to give that quality of balanced beauty and completeness termed classical.

The experienced arranger will see in the material to hand the possibilities of it. While looking at a branch of foliage, a certain line will dawn on you and as you start to trim and coax, the rhythm, that was perhaps only partially felt and not even understood, begins to take shape as the unwanted mass is snipped away to reveal the inate line.

Study these pages

and understand

good proportion

Good proportion is the first basic essential to remember. It pertains to one of the mathematical rules vital to any satisfactory design and is based on the relative height-to-width factor. It is achieved by measuring the container and ensuring that the overall height of the finished arrangement is, at least, one-and-a-half times to twice the measurement of the greatest dimension of the container, sometimes even higher. When cutting stems to place into an arrangement make sure that you leave enough to go into the container in addition to the visual portion required.

Generally, the fuller and more elaborate the arrangement, the higher it should be in proportion to the container. A tall person can always carry more width or girth than his shorter neighbour who must keep carefully to the essentially trim basic lines of the anatomy or he will look disproportionate.

The first arrangement is very good in itself consisting mainly of foliage. Canna leaves, variegated and plain phormium leaves and a monstera leaf together with two pampas grass heads are arranged in a diamond-shaped design but – and it is a very big but – the floral materials outweigh the comparatively small container. They are correctly related to each other but are out of proportion with the vase which is as lost beneath its burden as a child would be if he tried to carry his father.

The second picture reveals a fault but one erring on the right side. The strong, upthrusting lines of the dominant phormium and yucca leaves demand a generous height. Nevertheless, this is overdoing a good thing.

The vase on its own, without a base, is not man enough for the intended design. Even the small round base, which counts as part of the container but makes no aesthetic contribution to the embryo design, does not provide sufficient countermeasure to the extreme height of the foliage. This measures five-and-a-quarter times the height of the vase alone and four times the diameter of the base.

The base is surprisingly wider than the vase is tall by approximately a quarter so the measurement, by which the lengths of stems are gauged, must be taken across the diameter of the base because this is the greatest measurement of the two-part container.

In the third picture the height of the leaves has been reduced to only three times the height of the vase and two of the lower leaves have been removed to make the arrangement lighter in keeping with the reduced height. However, to make my point clear about the height to width proportion, I have bought into use a much larger, more solid-looking oakwood base which immediately dwarfs the height of the foliage.

The height of the leaves is now fractionally less than the width of the base, and the horizontally placed yucca leaf, although positionally correct, is vying with the upright phormium stem for the lead position. This arrangement is 'over-containered' and the height is overpowered and outmeasured by the overall width. It is very obviously wrong.

In the fourth illustration I have reverted to the height of the leaf in the second picture which measures five-and-a-quarter times the height of the vase. However, the width of the new base is such as to render the height of the tallest leaf just one-and-a-half times greater than the total width.

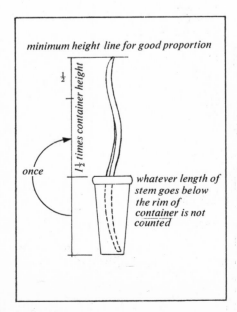

minimum height line for good proportion

$\frac{1}{2}$

$1\frac{1}{2}$ times container height

once

whatever length of stem goes below the rim of container is not counted

Here is the final result. Gladioli, each a
little deeper in colour than its neighbour,
descend to the palmate fatsia leaves at the
rim of the chased copper vase and make the
whole arrangement come alive. The brilliant coppery colourings of these lovely
blooms team up splendidly with all the
other components of this now well-
proportioned arrangement.

Be bold with height

Tuberoses have been one of my favourite
flowers since childhood. They are very
long-lasting and strongly and gloriously
scented. Although only native to warmer
climes, they are being imported on to the
London market and repay the little extra
cost involved.

A copper Persian water jug is the container for this arrangement which uses
three stems of elegant tuberoses. Phormium leaves establish the height of the
arrangement which is twice that of the tall
container. A minimum leaf height of one-
and-a-half times the jug's height would
have sufficed but with its broad girth the
extra height is better. You can see this for
yourself by placing your hand or a piece of
paper over the tops of the top three leaves.
The arrangement is still quite pleasing.
However, I hope you will agree that, when
you remove your hand or the paper, the
design gains from the extra height which
equates the eye with the broad girth.

The stems were held in place by crumpled
1½-in. mesh wire netting which was
fastened into the neck of the jug by an unseen twist around the handle. All the stems
were long enough to allow for the unseen
portions immersed within the vase. Some
of the material was secured with twists of
netting in the neck of the container with
stem length sufficient to drink the water.
Another way of overcoming the difficulty
of obtaining long enough stems for such a
tall container would be to fit a tin into the
neck of the jug. The tin could be buckled
over the rim of the jug and touched up
with matching copper paint.

Monstera leaves were taken from a
house plant. These last a long time when
cut and they contributed to an arrangement in perfect proportion and in consequence one which was beautiful and
thoroughly pleasing.

Bases in action

An attractive base can contribute greatly to the beauty of an arrangement. There can be all sorts of bases to vary the look of any one container and many containers for one favourite base – a veritable mix'n'match.

A very ordinary vase becomes an extraordinary one if combined with a suitable base. The base can either be unusual in its own right or possess some indefinable quality of unity with the container.

Bases can consist of anything from a large tough evergreen leaf to a humble burl of wood. They may be of somewhat more expensive origin like an artistic piece of ceramic. My own favourite is a lovely piece of water-green polished marble. The base in this arrangement is a simple but very elegant bamboo raft.

A base becomes part of a container not only aesthetically but practically, too, for determining the overall height of the arrangement. When using a tall container on a smaller base, the container is the yardstick on which you calculate your measurements for the arrangement because it has the greater dimensions. If, however, the base is greater in its largest dimension than the container, then the proportions of the arrangement are gauged by this.

In this arrangement, the bamboo base is the dominant factor. It is constructed in two parts but the measurement is taken along one section only. This is because it is not a solid oblong and the split base gives a receded line which the eye accepts for the basic height requirement.

The main flower stem and iris leaves rise to exactly one-and-a-half times the width of the raft base. They could be higher which would still look very attractive but with just a few flowers it looks better as it is. The minimum is absolutely necessary but a little extra according to the dictates of the vase and/or base can be just as good.

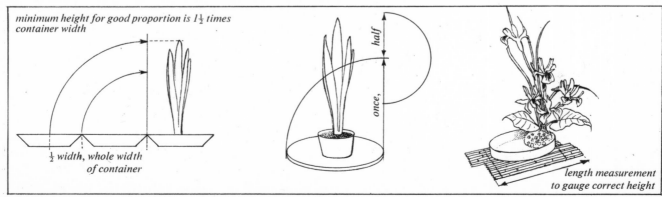

minimum height for good proportion is 1½ times container width

½ *width, whole width of container*

half

once,

length measurement to gauge correct height

Exceptions

prove the rule

Seeming exceptions to this basic height requirement occur occasionally when arranging flowers for a small dinner table or in pedestal-type containers. The varying heights of candlesticks and half pedestals have to be taken into account. In a full-sized floor pedestal, the main stem cannot be cut to measure one-and-a-half times the height of the pedestal column as one would be through the ceiling but good pleasing proportion is achieved for these big fellows as well as their smaller counterparts by cutting the longest lateral stems to measure between them one-and-a-half times or more the height of the pedestal column. (Each side is approximately three-quarters the height of the column.) In addition, they are sometimes positioned so that they sway gracefully towards the floor thus reducing, by optical illusion, the height of the column.

For most dining tables a bare minimum of one-and-a-half times the size of the greatest dimension of the container can be achieved and visibility maintained by selection of the right container which should be small or closely in keeping shape and sizewise with the table. If, however, the table is rather too small or narrow to provide a freeway of visibility above the flowers, allowing for the fact that when you are close to something it always appears bigger and taller, then apply the principle of pedestal-type proportion by either elongating an oval-shaped arrangement as shown in the colour illustration on page 37 for a long narrow table or, if using a small round container with a pedestal type of stem such as a fruit compote in which the overall height correctly proportioned would be too tall for your particular table setting, then reduce the overall height by gracefully trailing flowers and foliage over the rim of the container thus maintaining good proportion.

Candlestick

arrangement

Candlesticks can be treated in much the same way as pedestals although they are altogether smaller of course. Because they are smaller, they can be used proportion-

ately as any ordinary stereotyped container for there is no fear of raising the roof with the height. However, this would demand a tall narrow design, which, although very attractive indeed, would require firmer flowers than these lovely tulips.

Actually the tulips have already served an upright term of office when in their stiff flush of freshness and are now not so good at standing to attention. But why worry? There is much joy, and for many days yet, to be had out of their graceful bends so here they are in a fresh setting.

The china dolphin also seems very pleased with his catch of beautiful pale pink tulips arranged with just their own leaves curled back upon themselves to hide the cellular brick, and provide depth at the centre of the arrangement.

Reaching gracefully downwards, the two longest stems, each measuring approximately three-quarters the total height of this mini-pedestal container (approximately one-and-a-half times the height be-

tween them), provide the necessary proportion to offset the container's height.

The flowers are actually held in a candle-cup, obtainable from most florists and so useful for turning the top of a candlestick, bottle or narrow-necked vase into a manageable container.

These candlecups have already been shown in the previous chapter (page 20). The projection fits into the socket designed to take the candle and saturated cellular brick can be cut to a tight fit and away you go with flowers instead of candles, although a candle can be used, too, along with the flowers when it suits the arrangement. In this case, a hole will have to be cut in the cellular brick to allow the candle entry to its socket or wire netting can be used as an alternative means of holding the stems. It will help tremendously to secure the wire netting in position by slinging 'guy ropes' of rubber bands, in a colour matching the container, from the neck of the container to hook on to some cut ends of the netting.

A round arrangement for a round table

A candlecup within a bonbon dish or a wine glass minus its base could imitate this attractive and unusual flower holder. Keep good cut-glass wine glasses that have suffered the all-too-common fate of having their bases and lower stems broken. They will often come in useful to improvise a container. The broken stem end can be inserted firmly into a big wedge of Plasticine or contact cement.

The reduced main stem, a spray chrysanthemum, of this arrangement is inserted into the upper portion of this fountain container. Satisfying proportion is achieved nevertheless by reducing the optical height of the bonbon dish with delicately drooping stems flowing over the edge of the fountain so that everyone dining can see each other clearly over the flowers – a priority in any arrangement for a meal table.

Having established the height with the main flower, supporting shorter stems of spray chrysanthemums have been added amid delicate 'fillers' consisting of Queen Anne's Lace and dainty climbing geranium

flowers which soften the edge and complete this upper storey. Dainty chrysanthemum buds provide a gentle transition between the upper and lower tiers where more spray chrysanthemums circle three lily pips amidst a froth of Queen Anne's Lace with silver senecio foliage spilling over the bowl. This is a harmony in tints and tones of pinks and creamy white guaranteed to complement your guests.

In the colour plate on page 37, an elongated (extended side stems) oval arrangement maintains good proportion despite the reduced central height which had to be kept low because of the comparative narrowness of the long Sheraton table. When the table is fully extended I dramatise the sides still further.

Dainty flowers and foliage are necessary for table work. These airy-fairy arrangements often look more interesting and are easier to create with mixed flowers from the summer border and little, if any, foliage.

The reverse is true of the dramatic bold-contoured flowers, like my beloved strelitzias, which give of their best on their own in self-flower arrangements. For a pretty effect use mixed flowers. For a striking effect restrict yourself to one or, at most, two of a type.

Half pedestal

This half-pedestal vase is an excellent example of how the lateral stems can be extended to offset the height of the pedestal column.

Cut the pedestal in half by placing your hand, or, better still, a piece of paper on the picture. You now have a normal type of short pedestal bowl and you will see how the profuse arrangement of flowers with the extended lateral arms immediately becomes overpowering and out of proportion. The height is generously correct, but the side arms need to be drastically curtailed. Remove your hand or paper and view the arrangement as is and the whole thing becomes pleasing, although now it appears that the height is reduced. The measurement of the lateral arms together provide the correct proportionate relationship to the elongated pedestal. Each measures, from the rim of the container, the exact height of the pedestal so that between them they are twice the height of the pedestal. If they had drooped towards the table they would, of necessity, have been cut shorter for they would have overpowered the comparatively short pedestal column.

Dahlias, physostegia and belladonna lilies in shades and tints of mauve, mauve-pink and white – the white linking the flowers and container while their mauve-

pink throats blend with the other flowers –
make this diamond-shaped design a little
out of the ordinary, despite the fact that it
is basically a mass arrangement.

The water bowl, being possessed of both
a flat bottom and good depth, contains a
heavy pinholder with crumpled wire netting to secure the stems firmly in position.

Physostegia is commonly known as the
Obedient Flower. It is quite fascinating in
that each little individual floret can be
turned round upon the stem to face any
way you choose to place it.

Full length floor
pedestal

In the colour plate on page 37 is a pedestal
arrangement in a gorgeous mixture of
roses and bougainvillea. This daring combination of magenta and orange-red is
deeply satisfying. Flowering simultaneously in my Cape garden, substitutes can
be used for the bougainvillea in less
fortunate climates.

It is essential when arranging flowers on
a massed scale such as in full-sized pedestals that the actual water container is deep
enough to hold a great number of stems
and also wide enough to allow for free
circulation of air around them.

It must be flat based and heavy in itself
and, if possible, have a turned rim so that
large-sized thick rubber band 'guy ropes'
can nestle unobtrusively beneath the rim
for extra stability of the netting by taking a
four-way cross pull when you hook on the
cut ends of netting as shown in sketch
form.

The 1½-in. mesh wire netting could be
cut to measure perhaps six times the
square of the water area and placed, as
usual, ends uppermost.

Always use a big heavy pinholder and
contact cement to secure it in place. A
little contact cement on the outside of this
container will also prevent it slipping
around on the pedestal. A word of warn-
ing. Many adhesives spoil the surfaces of
containers so I would advise you very
strongly to buy a substance from a good
florist which is guaranteed harmless.

Full-sized pedestals, as I have already
explained, cannot obtain proportion by
the usual method of one-and-a-half times
the height of the greatest measurement of
the container because the tall pedestal
column is part of the container. In fact, it

is all that should show of the container for
the water bowl must be completely concealed to be correctly arranged and termed
a pedestal arrangement. Therefore, the

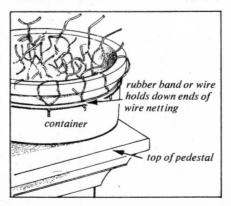

rubber band or wire
holds down ends of
wire netting

container

top of pedestal

lateral stems take over the proportionate
balance between them as with the candlestick and half pedestal already shown.
However, now they are exaggerated in a
downward sweep of graceful bougainvillea
to offset the height of this elongated
column and knock it back by optical
illusion.

All the foregoing seeming exceptions to
the general rule of proportionate cutting
have, in fact, still maintained the status
quo of proportion by virtue of two lateral
stems sharing the duty together in lieu of
the one upright stem in more conventional arranging.

Now we come to something definitely
different. No two stems combine to replace one in compensatory measurement.

The Orient differs

The Japanese, perpetrators of such exquisite floral art, show that a sufficiency of proportion can be achieved by measuring the depth plus width, and up to half again, of the container for their main stem – the heaven or shin line as it is called in the moribana style of arranging.

The secret behind this dictum lies in the fact that they use such few materials, stressing good clean line, with great simplicity and they lay emphasis on voids. Try using less than minimum height when using more material in a typical western style of arrangement and see how ill proportioned will be the unpleasing result.

This Keishin-kei – windswept arrangement – of flowering pine and arums is an example of the aesthetically satisfying quality of Japanese art.

To sum up

Occidental style of arranging generally calls for a minimum of one-and-a-half times the greatest dimension of the container with some certain exceptions detailed in this chapter.

Oriental arranging stresses a maximum of up to one-and-a-half times of any given container, again with exceptions varying with the school.

balance– aesthetical and practical

Good balance, apart from proportion, is an obvious essential in all art. In the art of flower arrangement, it is of practical as well as of aesthetic importance.

A third factor is the correct use of colour which plays a determining rôle. In fact, the way colour is used can put a design out of balance or it can, conversely, help to create a semblance of balance where none exists. Ideally it should be used to perfect an arrangement.

An arrangement of flowers, however well proportioned, must be correctly balanced or it will topple. If the lack of balance is not sufficient to actually make it insecure, it can still disturb the eye. When colour is used incorrectly, this will put the whole design out of gear and make it seem unbalanced although it may be quite stable physically.

In flower arranging we are dealing with colour all the time. It is essential to grasp the fact that dark colours along with round, solid flower and leaf shapes are used low down within an arrangement to anchor it and that the lighter colours and more delicate, tapering forms of flowers, buds, branches and foliage are arranged at the extremities. This is illustrated in the following two colour pictures.

The first is of a symmetrical pyramid design eminently suited to the shape of the gilt compote in which it is contained. The flowers are set well into the dish and are both physically and visually secure. Everything looks, and is, firmly in place with pleasing proportion and balance.

Rich flame red, apricot and yellow combine happily in an analogous colour scheme of well-balanced harmony. Bracken, carnations, gerberas and a deep apricot poppy give colour stability and depth where it is required at the base and these flowers also repeat and perfect the pyramid pattern of the overall design.

Within a background of deeper colour and flanked by creamy-yellow double stocks, a paler apricot poppy and a very light apricot gladiolus lead the eye out of this base pyramid of colour into the tapering height of fewer flowers, which are lighter in colour and more delicate in form with bromus grass and hemerocallis at the topmost extremity.

Fennel flowers and more day lilies outline the sides. New buds open on the day lilies as the originals fade and since they are on the outskirts they can be replaced with comparative ease.

The movement and good balance of the pedestal arrangement (page 37) circle out from a very dark and very large rose, centr-ally placed and set well into the container. If this flower protruded, its size and depth of colour would unbalance the arrangement.

This specimen rose is supported by a circlet of others in variety which gradually diminish in size and colour depth towards the apex. Trails of bougainvillea and variegated ivy complete an outer circle in matching tints and tones.

The whole arrangement is kept dainty in proportion to its slender height and to be in keeping with its elegant surroundings. To this end the bougainvillea has been considerably thinned otherwise the outline and arrangement generally would have been too massive and would have overpowered the marble column.

The dining-table arrangement, in a narrow, oval, pewter bowl, is composed of mauve and pink sweet peas and pink and white roses. The topmost roses are in bud and are the lightest in colour weight. Their height is the bare width of the container. This reduced height allows for easy conversation across the table and the elongated side stems of valerian compensate for this height reduction. The overall pattern of colour is deep at the centre base and the low sides with a considerable introduction of white at the top which emphasises the contour and provides a pleasing sense of colour balance.

Working with colour

Colour disposition is a vital factor in the good balance of an arrangement. Red, orange and yellow are the strong vibrant colours. They advance towards you and are exciting and warm. Violet, blue and green, the soft receding colours, are calming and cool. With black added to the pure hue we get shades and depth while the addition of white to the pure hue makes tints. A deep red rose commands the eye and appears so much heavier – you can almost wager that it weighs more than its pink counterpart while a white flower seems lighter still.

All the shades appear heavy visually and in addition the advancing triplet always clamour for attention. Therefore, if you place a flower which appears bigger and heavier because of its colour above a paler-tinted specimen, even though this lighter-coloured flower may be the same size or even bigger, the arrangement will become visually top heavy and out of balance.

Use the dominating shades at the base of an arrangement to provide weight anchorage whether it is a mixed colour arrangement, analogous or complementary, or a variety of shades, tints and tones in a self-colour harmony known as a monotone scheme. Graduate the colour depth from the base and centre outwards and upwards so that the colour intensities gradually become less towards the extremities.

Do not scatter colour. Always connect it by good transition and ensure an even disposition of colour depth on each side of an imaginary plumb line in symmetrical designs while asymmetrical designs are balanced by a heavier grouping of colour depth and size closer to the plumb line on one side. These sketches make this point clear. If all the available small flowers on long stems happen to be dark and the large flowers are short and light, as so often happens, cut some of the tall dark flowers shorter and group them artistically in the centre, backing them with some heavy foliage, if necessary, to overcome the difficulty.

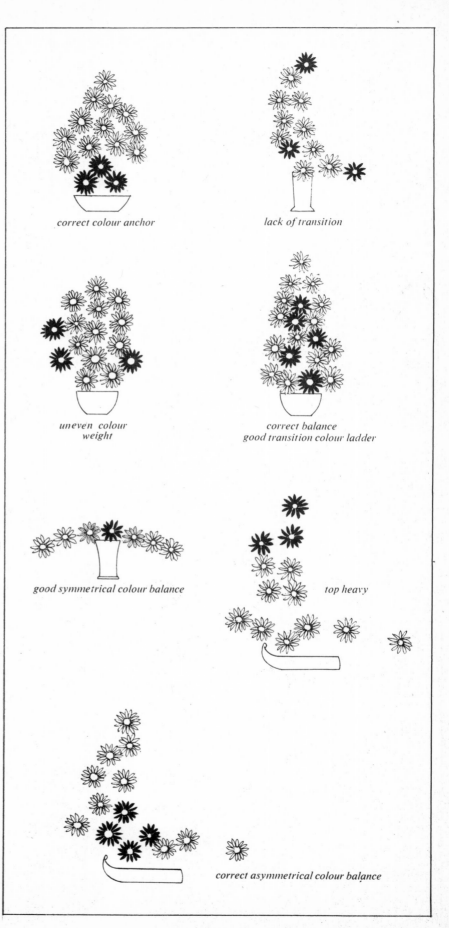

correct colour anchor

lack of transition

uneven colour weight

correct balance
good transition colour ladder

good symmetrical colour balance

top heavy

correct asymmetrical colour balance

Form balance

There are two kinds of form balance. These are symmetrical and asymmetrical.

In symmetrical balance, the main stem is placed centrally with an even distribution of material on each side of it. The general appearance is pleasing if somewhat static. Many different designs are possible in symmetrical form, however, with which to ring the changes, as will be seen throughout the book.

In asymmetrical balance, the main stem is placed to one side of the centre of the container. This placement is more obvious in oblong containers but holds good for all shapes be they urns, vases or even bottles. The main stem is supported by a secondary arm, which is cut shorter than the main stem, and this marks the horizontal line forming the width on the longest side. Heavier material is placed on the opposite side of, and close to, the main stem to balance the secondary stem rather as a flying buttress supports the high wall of a building.

You might think that this is a somewhat restricted shape. There is, in fact, a great feeling of movement and vibrant alertness in asymmetrical balance together with economy of material and a good variety of presentation.

In the following pages of this chapter, the photographs and line drawings present a visual explanation of the concept of these two form balances. To make it easy to follow I have created paired designs using the same flowers and containers on identical or very similar bases in each.

To sum up, balance falls into one of two general categories.

1 Balance is achieved by the weight being equally distributed on each side of an imaginary central line referred to as the plumb line. These are symmetrical arrangements.

2 Balance is achieved by conveying a visual effect of equal weight on each side of the plumb line even though both sides are irregular in form and shape. These are asymmetrical arrangements.

Always remember that the plumb line of balance relates directly to the centre of the arrangement itself and it is visualised as running straight through the focal point or heart of the arrangement.

An arrangement must be sure of itself. It must be capable of being moved without displacement of stems. This is achieved by ensuring that the container is stable and level, that the water holder or water-holding part of the container is flat and true, especially for bigger arrangements which require the firm placement of a heavy pinholder, and that the floral materials are firmly secured.

Bear in mind that the original stems which between them establish the skeleton or framework of a design should be so angled as to form a concave to allow room for the rest of the floral material to sit comfortably within the container.

Start your arrangement by positioning the main stem well back on the pinholder or in the wire netting, though not at the very back, allowing it to lean very slightly backwards. Then place the secondary stems so that they arise close from the first. Leave plenty of space in the middle of the container for subsidiary material and the focal point which must never unbalance the design by appearing to fall forward of the container, even though the design may call for a partial or complete concealment of the container.

I have written about the imaginary perpendicular line which divides an arrangement into two. The plumb line must dissect the centre of the actual arrangement itself, irrespective of the size and shape of the container and whether it stands on a base of any size or shape. In symmetrical arrangements, as shown here, there must be similar weight of like materials, both in colour and form, on each side of the plumb line. The main stem, therefore, in this arrangement of daffodils is placed at the centre back of the water holder.

A base is being used and so the arrangement has to be placed centrally on it. An equal amount of base must be visible on each side of the container when viewed from the front although the arrangement can be pushed to the back of the base.

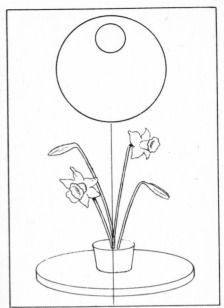

In the symmetrical design, the four fully opened central daffodils are evenly flanked by opening flowers and tight buds with soft flowing trails of pampas grass all held on a well-type pinholder upon an oval base.

The plumb line of balance running through the centre of the actual arrangement should occur to one side or the other of the water-holding container in an asymmetrical design. Should a base be used, as distinct from a Chinese-type stand of approximately the same base dimension of the container, the arrangement should be placed well to one side of it.

Here, a small water holder with a pinholder incorporated (a well pinholder) is concealed behind a piece of driftwood and placed to the extreme right of the elongated base. In asymmetrical arranging the components on each side of the plumb line can be very different but the overall picture must possess even weight of balance in both form and colour. To make this point quite clear, I have created this exuberant daffodil arrangement in which the bulk of the base and the winter branch balance the main body of flowers and foliage which the accompanying sketch will clarify.

The burgeoning branchlet, with last summer's leaf still bravely clinging, the driftwood and the base, a natural rough wood burl, balance the daffodils and their foliage and the two twiglets asymmetrically.

It is worth noting, too, that the pale honey-brown colour of the burl makes it appear lighter in weight so that the daffodils hold their own and are not overpowered by the base. This could have ruined the colour balance of the arrangement.

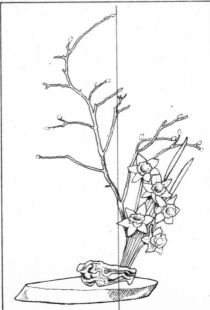

In this arrangement a bunch of ten tulips are arranged against a powerful background of two crinum lily leaves which rise sharply in the centre, supported by a couple of arum leaves springing laterally from the centre. The container is set centrally on an oblong cream base with a pinholder adhering firmly within the central socket of a muted black ceramic bowl. This forms a completely symmetrical background for these flowers.

The tulips are all of one colour and most of their leaves have been removed because they were weather damaged. They are divided equally on either side of the plumb line but are placed differently into the two halves of the design.

Starting at the top and working down with progressively shortened stems in the correct order of arranging we have the main, tallest stem (1) falling slightly to the right of the plumb line. This is closely followed by stem 2 to the left of the plumb line. Stems 3 and 4 have a greater divergence in height as they spread or fall away from the centre. Tulip 5 breaks step to add interest and to offset the expanse of unrelieved lily leaves. It is placed just fractionally left of the plumb line and is partnered by the shortest stem (6) which is an iota to the right of the line. Tulips 7 and 8 on the left balance 9 and 10 on the right. A few furled tulip leaves are used for depth in the centre of the design.

The cream-coloured oblong container is again upturned to do duty as a base and it has been paired by the same black ceramic bowl for the asymmetrical arrangement. Tulips have been used once more but there are only eight in this arrangement. The leaves are phormium and tulip.

The bowl is placed well to one side of the base and the main stem, a phormium leaf, swings up with a slight curve from as far right on the pinholder as it is possible to place it. It terminates just over to the left of the imaginary plumb line of balance.

Tulip 1 has been gently opened to reveal its beautiful markings and black stamens. It is supported by its own furled foliage to provide the necessary weight. The foliage also conceals the pinholder. Flowers 2 and 3 are asymmetrically balanced by their long arm opposites, tulips 4 and 5. Numbers 6, 7 and 8 are cut shorter and are angled to complete a swinging curve. They also act as fillers in an arrangement in which those flowers and upright phormium leaves that are close to the plumb line balance, or buttress if you prefer, the strongly outswinging phormium leaf and tulips plus the length of the oblong base.

design – the middleman between you and your materials

Design in flower arrangement is an original idea of dual parentage, sired by a multitudinous selection of containers – naturalistic and household – and born out of nature's bounty – various flora and minerals. Inspiration and the sure way to create beauty springs from these. When the latent art form found in the natural twists and striking forms of growth and mineral formation are coupled with the individuality of the arranger's imagination, attractive and very often unusual designs are created.

Line is the basic factor of any good design. Too often mass material or colour are the predominating values but these should be used discriminately and should be subordinate to a strongly emphasised lineal form.

All art is subject to basic principles which govern design and in this chapter, which combines the preceding fundamentals or principles of proportion and balance already stressed, I share with you the creative ideas which give rise to design and show their practical application.

Focal point

The axis or focal point of emphasis is of the utmost importance for around it the arrangement revolves. All the stems should meet neatly at the base of the arrangement like the spokes of a wheel centring on the hub. It is often expedient to focalise interest at this point, to give emphasis to the arrangement and to add base weight or anchorage. Additionally this focal point placement, as it is called, helps to conceal the basic mechanics such as the wire netting and pinholder or any other aid.

In the arrangement of proteas, the focal point is dramatised by twin king proteas held on a strong pinholder within a small tin fitted in the base of the driftwood itself. Immediately behind the driftwood is another small water container synchronised with the first so that they blend into one. Together, they are concealed by a collar of protea foliage and two embryo cycas palm leaves which flow out in support of the 'kings'. This allows the observer to see only one focal point, as is intended, from the centre of which emerges the unusual piece of driftwood accompanied by the *latifolia* proteas. A bud and graceful downward curving flower are raised to this height by the aid of a florist's horn or stem holder which is spliced on to a piece of reed to enable it to stand firm on the pinholder.

Line is the skeleton of good design

Line is the bone structure of flower arrangement. Dress it up for a fulsome mass arrangement if you want a lavish display of many flowers and much colour or pare it to the minimum by using just one flower and two or three beautifully elegant leaves. You can incorporate a piece of nature's own sculpture, driftwood, to provide the necessary height when arranging a minimum of material. However, whatever the design, do set a good, determined clean line and keep within its definition, then you will come up trumps each time.

There is nothing so disappointing as a hit and miss success. Your sense of the artistic may lead you to a lovely arrangement which pleases you and wins the admiration of all-comers. Then the next arrangement is a flop because the basic fundamentals are not really appreciated or understood.

In addition to the basic fundamentals which are dealt with chapter by chapter you must remember to:

1 Give your design sufficient, even generous, height as dealt with in the proportion chapter.

2 All stems must radiate from a hub or axis at the base of the design. This becomes the focal point of emphasis which arrests the eye and leads it into and through the whole design.

3 Cut the stems to different lengths and place them in the arrangement so that they are angled on separate planes. Each flower head or major component should be clear of its neighbour.

4 Trim twigs and remove fussy growth. This is especially applicable to shrubs in order to avoid ugly cross stems.

5 Swing the secondary and tertiary placements gently in a forward embracing curve to provide three-dimensional depth.

You do not have to be clever to achieve good design. To think this way is quite erroneous. A simple asymmetrical design even without any dual movement is always pleasing when inspiration will not come or when there are no unusual materials to inspire you.

Bear in mind the primary principles

especially those of proportion and balance and the five guiding rules enumerated on the previous page. These are grist to the mill. Take them to heart to make sure that you will never come unstuck. They can only rarely be broken and then you must be very sure of yourself. One can only break a rule when one is master of the subject.

When faced with flower heads like nerines and agapanthus, whose own rather floppy strap foliage does not really aid the arranger, you have a choice of two alternatives. You can either mass them in a conventional fan or pyramid contour design relying solely upon colour or you can thoughtfully separate a few flowers, with suitable foliage, which will have greater line impact. Here you see the result of the latter choice – an arrangement, to all intents and purposes, without a container.

Two aralia leaves form a base in lieu of a visible container and, from the overall width of their combined spread, the correct proportion is ascertained and maintained by the main stem which is a leaf from the *Strelitzia albus* tree, a giant member of the banana family. This young leaf was cut and left soaking in a bath for three days. It was then secured to a pinholder in water where, within a few hours, it curled to assume this shape. After this it served in a number of arrangements for over two months. A transitional link between the substantial form of the strelitzia leaf and the comparatively dainty flowers is effected by the introduction of the sturdy but smaller iris foliage.

All the stems converge to a central meeting point which the eye accepts, although it cannot see, beneath the base leaves because the directional line is obviously correct and, for that reason, eminently pleasing. Just refer this arrangement back to the guide lines. Each flower occupies its own individual plane (3) with no haphazard crossing lines (4). By careful angling of the stems, depth and a well-rounded contour prevail rather than a flat plane (5). The base leaves are also set on different planes.

all stems start from one point

Daffodils

cock-a-hoop

Although the daffodil foliage maintains an upright perpendicular line, the main movement is a jubilant hoop or, as it is shortened one side, a hook might describe it better. This is executed by the dominant daffodils around their foliage.

The narcissus family contains some lovely species but from the flower arranger's point of view they are difficult to work with and to incorporate into new designs. Most of the time we do not try very hard to think of new ideas as, with the arrival of the daffodils, we are so pleased to know that spring is coming after a bleak winter and a surfeit of chrysanthemums.

This design, quite correctly, is in keeping with the strait-laced upright mode of growth of these flowers and yet, with a little imagination, it has achieved distinction. It was necessary to cut the stems drastically in order to space the flower heads in this manner. I also utilised the slight variations in the size of the blooms so that the smallest were placed highest. In fact, the topmost flower has only just lifted its head from its swan neck bud formation.

Wire netting, measured around the outside of the copper mug after the style of 'once round your fist for your stocking size', holds the stems in place.

The metal container used in this arrangement breathes and is, therefore, sensibly allied to these early flowers. The slight transpiration of the container tends to lower the water temperature and this offsets, to some extent, the exhausting atmosphere of a heated room and gains for the daffodils a stay of execution which coal fires and central heating tend to inflict too speedily.

The self-contained circle

The copper bowl with dahlias is another example of an instant and long-lasting arrangement for busy people. The design plays upon a circle. The circle epitomises completeness, containing within itself the beginning and end of everything and gives the beholder a sense of satisfaction. It is abundantly manifest in nature. Just look around and see how many flowers are circular in overall formation.

Dahlias are deservedly such popular flowers and they belong to the daisy genera, the largest in the floral family tree. I have used just three in a pink colour to emphasise the roundness of the beautiful copper bowl, one of my treasures presented to me by Rhodesia.

Strips of cane have been bent into attractive curves and a trail or two of variegated ivy repeats these curves and brings the eye through from start to finish at the focal point.

Beautiful flower arrangements throughout the home need not cost much in money or time. There are plenty of garden flowers and many more which can be easily bought. By experimenting you can discover how effective the same flowers can look when arranged differently in varied designs. The exotic flowers may not be grown locally and can be expensive, especially in temperate climates where they have to be imported, but as they last so much longer than the more ordinary flowers, they often work out cheaper and they are time-saving into the bargain. Because of their definition of form, they are almost as beautiful in continuous use as dried material.

A square but it is modern

This arrangement was evolved in response to the strong movement of the driftwood. This is a lovely bit of ironwood hailing from the vicinity of World's View, the burial place of Cecil Rhodes in Rhodesia. It is very hard and heavy and I wore it round my neck, for lack of a better place, while flying back to England. What a dedicated arranger will do! It was well worth it, however, and is still much treasured and admired. Together with just three phormium leaves, which differ from the more usual in possessing graceful twists, it forms a long-lasting outline arrangement to escort a few or more flowers.

Two bent gladioli, kinky seconds, were especially selected for their shape to form a square along with the L-shaped driftwood. The taller spike with the exaggerated movement runs parallel with the base of the square outlined by the driftwood. The shorter spike provides visual balance and picks up the directional line seen in the focal point of the gnarled wood.

The empty space or void in this design is of the utmost importance for it accentuates lineal direction and arrests interest on the square.

Cross out

the mediocre

The home-made container is fashioned from mixed shells. It is very dainty and suggested itself as the ideal container for these very delicate, shell-like flowers which are members of the protea family. I call the container platypus and if you have ever seen this strange little animal with its flat feet, you will understand why. It was the flat feet formed by the scallop shells which suggested the cross line of this arrangement – a design which admirably suits the five stems of flowers. These flowers are botanically *Serruria florida* but they are more usually known by the common name of Blushing Brides because their centres are blush pink fading to the softest creamy white and they are also inclined to shyly hang their faces.

Like most spray flowers they have to be used as they grow, for the florets have so little length of individual stems that they are almost useless separated from the group. For this arrangement I needed to do very little trimming of excess florets, only enough to promote good line by reducing the bulk which also enabled the stems to hold their heads a little higher. Unwanted florets, if left, would have presented a square blob instead of, as now, a semi point.

Some dainty wild grass – broom would have been equally suitable – softens the main cross movement by supporting it within an overall pyramid or symmetrical triangle. However, the cross is the main design and this is therefore made to stand out in relief.

Circle of eternity

King proteas are such outstanding flowers. Beautiful is too inadequate a word to describe them and magnificent only begins to do them justice. One of these flowers is virtually an arrangement in itself and so this design is based on, and revolves around, this bold circular flower. The container had to complement the protea, both in shape and colour, and so this dark green glass floating bowl was the choice. This is circular in shape to be in keeping with the flower.

Two sisal leaves, which are so heavy that they almost bend over with their own weight into graceful curves as they grow, were encouraged into this mode by having their tips pressed back on to the pinholder to look like a huge bow. These elliptical curves, being segments of a circle, serve a dual purpose. They are closely identified with the bold circular movement of the bowl and the flower and they provide a transition between these complete circles and the vertical line introduced by the equally bold sansevieria and phormium. This foliage forms a right angle which strikes into the heart of the main circular movement introducing a feeling of vigour and heightening the interest. It also provides the necessary height to offset the width of the bowl.

This is another arrangement which can be left in continuity for as long as you like to have it around. The protea will eventually fade but it takes on another beauty. With the exception of the phormium, which can easily be replaced, the greenery, including the collar of protea leaves, will stay as fresh as the proverbial daisy. There is also a bonus attached. Both the sansevieria and sisal will develop roots in water and can be planted in pots or in the garden, depending on where you live, when the arrangement is dismantled.

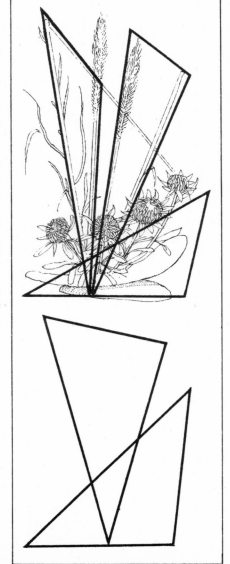

The ubiquitous triangle is provocative

Ship ahoy! De-prickled prickly pears were the instigators of this arrangement which conveys the illusion of a ship carrying a cargo of waratahs. Stripped bamboo (arundinaria) has been bent to represent the rigging but as I did not want to carry the impression too far by being over authentic, I have purposely turned my ship back to front. This allows me the licence of introducing other factors, such as the bamboo flower spikes, without being hauled up before a sailing committee!

With this apology to yachtsmen, we can dissect the design and discover a number of triangles within the main scalene triangle which is the primary outline of this design, shown clearly in the accompanying sketches.

Triangles are aesthetically satisfying especially asymmetrical triangles which offer more interest by their irregularity than all the elliptical forms. These, as I have already said, hold the eye from start to finish in one sweep without calling for any effort from the onlooker. The ubiquitous triangle intrigues and holds the attention for much longer. The more you look, the more you perceive. If you check yourself when you like a particular design, you will realise why you like it. This is because you are looking at it with new eyes – eyes which are open to the hitherto unappreciated secrets of design.

Arrangements such as this last for weeks without a change of flowers. Waratahs are so long-lasting but where they are not available, well-formed disbudded chrysanthemums make good substitutes and are satisfyingly durable although they cannot be compared with the keeping qualities of the waratahs.

Always remember to use weight in size of form and, of course, colour at the base of an arrangement and to graduate (transition) from there upwards and outwards.

It is important to defoliate flower stems partially or sometimes completely. This is to promote an uncluttered line and it also cuts down on the amount of water lost by the flowers through transpiration especially during hot weather or in heated rooms thus prolonging their lives.

Diagonals
are strong and lively

The diagonal is a line midway between the vigorous thrust of the vertical and the becalming horizontal. It is a very natural line for it almost creates itself from ordinary materials immediately to hand. It does not require outstanding curves, either natural or fashioned, nor does it demand much imagination. It does, however, need a tallish container, technically known as a vase, to give clearance for the descending arm.

The only time it can be employed satisfactorily in a flat container is when this is positioned on the edge of a mantelpiece or similar piece of furniture for the downward sweep will then flow clear over the edge.

Greeny-yellow spider chrysanthemums and three leaves of the acanthus plant, so beloved by sculptors and all artists, combine with a softly gilded metal urn in a classic arrangement. The largest, strongly centred flower is positioned as the focal point. It arrests the eye and conveys it to the topmost flower. From there the viewer is taken down the upper curving acanthus leaf on the right to the lowest flower and from here the eye is directed back into the centre by the lower acanthus leaf. There is no back view to this arrangement. The line is clearly seen at every angle of approach.

All the chrysanthemums were cut to different lengths and are quite clear of

each other. All the stems are cleanly angled to the centre with no criss-crossing of lines and they are held within $1\frac{1}{2}$-in. mesh wire netting crumpled into the urn and concealed by the foliage.

There are three categories of arranging and these restrict or liberate design.

Arrangement

The word arrangement conveys a group of flora – fresh, dried or preserved – within a single container unit of any size, type or shape. A typical arrangement is that of the spider chrysanthemums on this page. There are no extras. Everything is within one simple but attractive container. Sometimes a base can be included if it is genuinely seen to be part and parcel of the container as in the arrangement of proteas on page 41.

Composition

This allows scope to include all manner of extras, and imagination is given freer rein. Two arrangements can be linked together. Stones or drapes could be introduced and figurines or any other accessories can be used. To illustrate composition, I refer you back to the arrangement on page 9 and also to the one on page 8 where the bamboo container on a bamboo tray link up with the Chinese figurine in an eastern composition.

Interpretative

Interpretative designs can be arrangements but they are more usually compositions. They allow full rein to the imagination and can be great fun. They must convey a message to the viewer and the story must speak for itself.

Easter morning

Within the limited confines of the photograph, I am perforce using only four components to interpret Easter. Nevertheless, it is clear that the Madonna is descending a pebble-strewn path leading down to the sepulchre and has paused beside the stone rolled from its entrance. Above her are some 'lilies' she has passed.

Arums are not true lilies but they are commonly considered so and as such are always in demand at Eastertime in the northern hemisphere. These lovely and unusual arums can grow as tall as a person with spathes of a most beautiful green flushed white in the centres.

This design is alive with movement. The eye is primarily held by the stone which is, of course, the crux of the story. Hence it is used as the focal point supported by the black pebbles. As the eye rises from the stone, it meets the truncated stems leading to the lower arums. From these it ascends along the main stem, drops onto the curving stem beneath and returns in a sweep in imitation of the Madonna via the pebbles to the stone. There should be this element of movement in all good designs be they arrangements, compositions or interpretative designs. The fewer the materials, the better the effect.

Fan the dahlias

Two cotton palms can form a striking background for very few flowers and they triggered off the idea for this design. They are such perfect natural fans that I placed them as though they were two artificial fans, asymmetrically one above the other. Their stem ends meet firmly on the pinholder.

The dahlias form a design within a design. They contribute an upward thrust which contrasts and yet compliments the elliptical contour of the fans. A direct upward movement would have proved too much of a contrast and so I weaved the larger decorative dahlias subtly upwards to create a sinuous line which is taken up and completed by the smaller and taller pompons.

rhythm and repetition for a double punch

Rhythm and repetition are an integral part of good design. In all the arts rhythm is of immense importance. The painter cleverly uses light and shadow to draw the eye of the observer into and around his picture and the architect designs buildings with pleasing lines, which, although they are constructed of necessity, never fail to delight.

Of the three elements in music, too, melody and harmony take second place to rhythm which is basic and the most important. Rhythm is the ebb and flow of successive movements, best visualised as the ripple of ripening corn flowing before the summer wind, undulating without any irritating discontinuation. By clever transition of colour, the basic rhythmic sweep of a good design is intensified.

Repetition pinpoints this rhythm and draws attention to it. If you were creating a pretty curving S-bend arrangement, you could dramatise the centre of the design by fashioning a similar smaller S there. The S-bend is commonly known in flower arranging circles as the Hogarth curve after the famous painter of that name who made this beautiful shape peculiarly his own even to the point of signing his paintings on a miniature palette of like shape. The repetitive S is no more essential to the actual construction of the design than the sweet course is to the main course at dinner but, as sweet-toothed readers will agree, it does something for you. Likewise, subtle repetition does something for a good design of flowers and it can be achieved in many ways as you will see. It helps to focalise the eye so that it can swing smoothly through the whole design.

A fillip of colour can draw attention to an attractive feature if it is skilfully repeated. An unusual shape or design can be inspired, perhaps, by a lucky find of driftwood or suggested by an attractive piece of fungus collected from a tree in the woods. Looking for and collecting lovely bits and bobs can be a fascinating pastime. The strong lines of a more commonplace type of container can be repeated to great effect by a repetitive dominant movement within the design of the arrangement. A motif on a container can be repeated by echoing the types of flowers and colourings comprising the motif.

Accessories are helpful

Another way of achieving repetition is by the use of an accessory. This can serve to indicate or to highlight the main movement of a design like the upward sweep of the sweet peas on page 8 and the waratahs on page 58. Even more important, it can serve to complete a design, giving it stability and balance which it would otherwise lack. In this arrangement of orchids, the burgeoning branch plays a dominant role. The tropical orchid, being an epiphyte, needs a tree to sustain it, and, although these orchids were pot grown, a branch is the right consort for them in an arrangement. I purposely exaggerated the movement of the branch extending it well beyond the limits of good balance because I had an accessory in mind.

The two leather-bound books were placed horizontally beneath the branch to balance it and to add their classic beauty to that of the flowers and the polished antique table. The deep perpendicular folds of the drapes behind the composition give strength, by repetition, to the simple copper vase and effect a link between the arrangement and the accessory. The result of removing the books and the curtain folds is that the eye is left uncertainly teetering on the extreme edge of the branch. Replace the books and the drapes and the eye travels happily down the branch to the base of the vase and up again to the focal mass of flowers at the rim of the container thus completing a pleasing rhythmic exercise.

The next colour illustration is full of punch and movement. The strelitzias and their leaves along with dried cycas fronds are arresting in their simplicity. The up-sweeping diagonal movement tells the story that these floral birds were disturbed while drinking at the pool.

Figurines are the usual accessories for flower arrangements although the lids of boxes or other articles which are used as containers, attractive lids of compotes, some of which may incorporate a figurine handle, books, ash trays or even, occasionally, a pair of glasses or dainty binoculars can be used. The last mentioned can be part of a sporting composition to accompany suitably selected materials, and this is where we must pause to consider these so-called additions.

An accessory correctly used is most certainly not an addition. If it appears so,

then it is not essential to the design and must be removed. If, on the other hand, the arrangement seems to be lacking something without it, it should be replaced and the plant material should then be checked for superfluities and these should be eliminated instead.

Borrow rhythm
from a figurine

Vertical figures, like the Easter Madonna of the interpretative design on page 52, are often used as a substitute for an important line, as indeed they should be because of their dominance and/or their religious connotations. In fact, this particular composition was built round and designed for the accessory which was the basis of the composition, the reason for it and the essence of it and the plant material repeated its rhythmic line.

Horizontal accessories, like books and small complete seated figures, are not so dominant but they are just as important if used correctly. The great thing is to ensure that your choice of accessory is in sympathy with the other components. It should not jar the sensibilities but should contribute a double punch of repetitive rhythm.

However you choose to use the fundamental of repetition, do remember it is important to stop at just the right moment so that you do not spoil the effect by overdoing it. Remember the bore you know who repeats all his jokes ad infinitum.

This discrete emphasis is explained and clearly shown in the following arrangements and, in some cases, the line drawings accompanying the arrangements. All in all, subtle repetition within good design is the keynote of beautiful arranging with a difference.

Arrangement
versus composition

As I have said before, accessories are helpful. They can assist in promoting rhythm and give scope for delightful pleasing repetition. However, there are other means of accentuating rhythm and repetition within the actual arrangement without the need for a more effusive composition. For a refresher turn back to page 51.

Form and colour
for repetitive play

Containers and materials should be chosen with an eye to each other. Something in one should ring a bell and assist you to select the other.

When I did this arrangement, time was very limited and the florist a good few miles away. The garden was between seasons and offered very little except for the intrepid day lilies. These have colour and line but they usually only last for a day, hence their nickname. They do open new buds each morning even when cut but as these, more often than not, upset the line of the design, the arrangement has to be altered drastically.

On this account, an elaborate arrangement was out of the question – simple and quick was the answer. I selected just four stems of hemerocallis, eight flowers, for this arrangement with just an oblong pinholder to hold them securely. Apart from some papyrus, there was no other foliage.

How was I to make the most of this material? My eye fell on this wooden Balinese figure. From it I got my cue and found an obvious link. The similarity of form between the lilies and the boy's headdress was striking – a likeness which was underwritten, too, by their colouring – the rich wood-brown shading on the lighter flower petals and the burnished wood colour of the darkest couple of flowers. So I achieved a repetitive play of form and colour between the two components. Each flower head stands on a separate plane so that they can be seen clearly and definitely as befits their sculptured form.

I positioned the figure directly in front of a small water-holding pinholder so as to hide it and utilised the natural curves of the stems so that they moved with each other without any criss-crossing. The two most curvaceous stems were kept at full length to establish sufficient height for generous proportion and they swing down to meet their partners, at the base of the dagger, with a carefree swagger. Here they are all met by the papyrus which serves to accentuate the rhythm.

Complementary rhythm in a static decorative feature

There is a strong and obvious repetition of the growth rhythm between the living flowers and those in the Indonesian plaque. When this simple arrangement stands in our hall, it brings forth much comment because both the real and the metal flowers seem identical.

Other flowers, in place of the waratahs, can be used when in season like chrysanthemums and cactus dahlias, both of which identify with the plaque flowers. This wall piece does, therefore, decorate our hall for much of the year although its place is sometimes taken by a Chinese plaque with which I team another arrangement. As space is usually limited in halls and there often is not much room for a big display, clever utilisation of wall space to combine with an arrangement of moderate size can result in an imposing sight.

Team up a landscape picture in which trees play a prominent part so that you select a beautiful living branch or piece of driftwood as the main theme of your design and follow the same rhythmic movement of the picture. If there is water in your painting, repeat and emphasise that feature in your arrangement. Create or cause the rhythm of your design to project that of the picture.

Waratahs resemble chrysanthemums in shape. They are both also very woody and extremely long-lasting but there the resemblance stops. Whereas you could almost sit on a waratah and get the worst of it, the temperamental chrysanthemum drops all its petals and leaves you with a forlorn stalk if you even so much as brush against its delicate sensitivity. However, they share an uncompromising stiffness of stem and we cannot twist and curve the stems as the metal artist has fashioned those in the plaque. Flowers with a 'heel' or, in other words, offshoots from a natural break, however, enable you to achieve some movement, as I have here, and the eye, with a little artistic licence, allows us to get away with it.

The accompanying sketch traces the reverse movement of the dual stems so as to show the rhythm more clearly by isolating the stems.

Rhythmic
tangle of triangles

Repetition is the obvious feature of this stark line arrangement. See how many triangles you can spot. These magnificent flowers, which look as though they had been sculptured in alabaster, rank high among my favourites because, beauty apart, they set a line for an arrangement. Take your cue from the way they point and encourage their upright but very pliable stems to follow their own line. Do not crowd them.

To encourage a stem to bend the way you want it to, maintain a firm but gentle pressure on it as you stroke it into a curve. If the stems are very thick and luscious, carefully peel a thin strip from the base of each upwards which will make them more pliable.

While discussing the mechanics of behind-the-scenes know-how, I will just mention that because the container is a shell, with a typically curving inside, it is almost impossible to use a pinholder. I have crumpled wire netting inside the shell and this remains in place almost all the time. It is only removed very occasionally for a thorough spring clean which is all that is necessary if you keep the water sweet day by day. The less the netting is moved, the less the shell interior is likely to be scratched.

For all delicate stems, plastic brick is the ideal within this container but arums are too heavy for the relatively small amount of brick to be able to cope satisfactorily and fleshy stems, as I have mentioned previously, do not take kindly to this medium. Other stems, like carnations, love it.

Stark line arrangements and arums are synonymous. These flowers are completely out of place huddled together in any typical container for each flower is a line study in itself. They must be used sparingly and in countries where they are an expensive luxury, such as at Eastertime in England, this factor alone is a boon.

This particular arrangement is a rhythmic evolution of triangles. There are five of them and, if you consider the shape of the flowers themselves, yet another two making seven. The third arum is curved so that it presents itself as a trapezium and has to be counted out. The marble base is the first and basic triangle. The two graceful philodendron leaves, in association with the base, form two more triangles.

The three arums together, standing above the leaves, make the fourth triangle while the completed arrangement presents the all-encompassing fifth triangle.

Finally, and this point is explained more fully in chapter six, I draw attention to another feature contributing to this arrangement. This is the tranquil association of the natural shell container set upon the cool green watery-looking marble base along with the creamy arums whose natural habitat is damp underfoot although they like their heads in the sun. Also notice the smooth transition of scale and texture between all the components of this fascinating repetitive design.

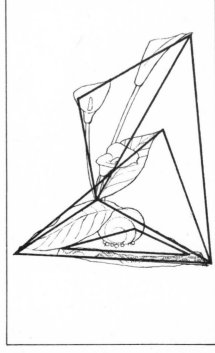

Quiet rhythmic beauty

This arrangement is based on the simple clean line of the brass vase with three main contributory factors. You may have a vase like this at home or you can often pick one up inexpensively in one of those fascinating, lesser breed of antique shops – a visit which adds purpose to many a country drive.

In itself the container is nothing to shout about except for the quiet rhythmic beauty inherent in the pear shape, loved and used by nature itself. Look at a map of the world and notice how most land masses end in a variation of the upturned pear as they dip to the South Pole.

The overall design of the arrangement focuses upon a repetition of this elementary shape with an exaggerated height to assist to that end. Do not forget the extra length of stem required for the unseen inside of the tall vase.

With vase and design in repetitive accord, the choice of the flowers and foliage is of paramount importance in the successful execution of the idea. Kniphofia flowers, red-hot pokers, resemble the pear shape and growing as they do, beyond and seemingly independent of their own strap-like foliage, the sleek stems, selected for their own slight curves do not require any accompanying foliage when arranged. This would only serve to hide the stems which are required to perpetrate the design. A whorl of poinsettia leaves, chosen because they sufficiently resemble the individual florets of the kniphofia flowers, complete the arrangement at the focal point, consolidating interest at the influx of stems into the container and concealing the wire netting which firmly holds the materials in the vase.

This is a simple arrangement but, as always, simplicity requires careful thought. It is absolutely necessary that all the components are in concert with each other. Here it is the similarity in shape between the container and flowers which achieves the harmony in the rhythm of the design.

A scoop of a container

Curves are the order of the day here. The possibilities of the homely colourful geraniums are often overlooked and this is a shame because their brilliant colourings and precise form are well worthy of a sojourn in the home.

Walking through our orchard, my husband spotted this piece of driftwood – a fruit branch. He is a wonderful 'spotter'. I do not know whether he trained me or I trained him. Anyway, together we have found some treasures and you can, too, as long as you look with keen and perceiving eyes.

This piece looked most unassuming until I allocated it to the right container and contributory flowers. Our daughter, Zarmony, sent us the unusual container from Islamabad, Pakistan, as an anniversary present. All the family has been roped in, or should I say tuned in, to the fascinating art of using flowers, beautifully and originally. As soon as the gift was delivered, I determined that this traditional copper utensil must be given a place of honour in this book.

It has been fashioned in beaten copper, in a primitive manner, for two essential purposes. It can be used as a water scoop by pilgrims bathing in the Ganges and other waters or a wick can be run through the handle end to float in oil and so provide light in the humble home.

With the container's original uses in mind, the piece of driftwood repeats and emphasises the gradual upward curving rhythm of the water scoop-cum-oil lamp. The fruit branch sweeps upwards to end with a flourish just over the tip of the topmost and daintiest geranium and so carries the curve to a happy conclusion. It provides height and returns the eye down through the flowers to the two shortest which, along with some geranium foliage, mark the focal axis from where all the stems spring secured on an oblong pinholder.

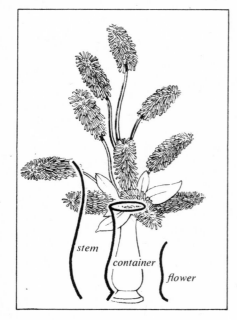

stem
container
flower

Doubles are
fun – two-into-one

Here is an original and unusual composition. The rhythmic movement passes between two separate arrangements, to and fro, like a good pass in rugger or soccer, to win through to ultimate success. Starting with the footwork of the containers, the teamwork continues throughout the different media of flowers, colour and mental image which conceived this whole set up.

Unlike the previous interpretative design, the Madonna on page 52, which was composed within a single flower arrangement, we now have two separate flower arrangements linked into one unit by 'swirling water'.

Living Waters could be the title of this picture and it all started with the lovely earth-coloured, leaf-shaped 'pool' container lined in palest aquamarine. I was aching to use this along with some smooth white, sea-washed pebbles picked off the beach. I have used this 'leaf' before (page 30) but see the difference now when used with imagination.

The larger arrangement is a simple upright set to one side of the pool container to give asymmetrical balance. This is quite pleasing in itself but nevertheless very ordinary. It became imaginatively different when a few left-overs of Queen Anne's Lace from another arrangement were placed in their dolphin container. The dolphin was placed at the edge of the pool to represent a fountain out of which pours fresh water. Queen Anne's Lace is a very apt medium to represent frothing water and eucomis sprays became the overflowing waters of the fountain. A ripple can even be discerned on the face of the water, lapping against the sides, caused by the forward flow of the current.

The pebbles, beside the pool, walk the eye up to the fountain and carry it round the curve of the dolphin. From there it moves down with the eucomis into the bottom of the pool and is led by more pebbles to the tall tranquil arrangement. This appears as at home at the end of this pool as in the shallows of my garden pool from where the white flowers and soft green foliage were cut.

You will notice how the swirling movement is continued within this arrangement which is lapped by the water as it flows from the fountain to cause the attractive twist discernible in the folds of the foliage which wraps itself around each tuberose separately. A spiralling rhythm has been created which is very calming and typical of anything to do with flowing water.

Although there are two focal points in a dual design such as this, the secondary axis is played down and there is a strong lead via the eucomis and pebbles into the tall primary arrangement so that the eye accepts the whole as one and enjoys what it sees in the double take.

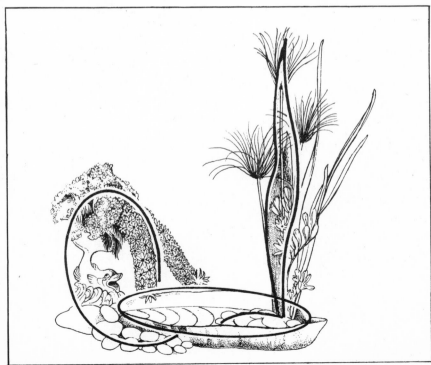

Identical twins

linked to form a

Gothic arch

Contrary to what you might at first imagine, doubles are wonderful material savers – real economy products in fact. You generally require less of everything and finish with more to show for what you do use. The excellence of such arrangements is dependent on voids. Although true of all arrangements, it is especially important here that it is not so much what you put in that counts but what you leave out. They also appreciate a clear uncluttered background and some elbow room.

There is no subordinate arrangement here. A pinholder in each of this pair of cream ceramic oblongs holds identical material – variegated flax and pampas grass with its own foliage. It is purely a composite of two arrangements pertaining to one design. It does not set out to present a story or to depict anything in particular but as I worked each arrangement towards its twin, a rhythmic perpendicular arch appeared as I followed the 'feel' of the materials. From an identical repetitive pair of stark vertical designs, a complementary arching movement evolved by means of the curling pampas grass to soften the composition.

A piece of seaweed, completely encircling the front arrangement, follows the lead of the arch to forge a further link between the dual participants. It directs the eye back to the one at the rear. Black water-washed pebbles, apart from concealing the pinholder, form a connecting link in repetition between the arrangements.

Something

to crow about

This cocky little cockerel has been promoted from being just a gay ornament to an important accessory whose strong linear form suggests and controls the whole design.

He high-steps his way through a colourful array of spring flowers arranged with some cytisus which has been persuaded into a shallow crescent in repetition of the cockerel's own jaunty carriage.

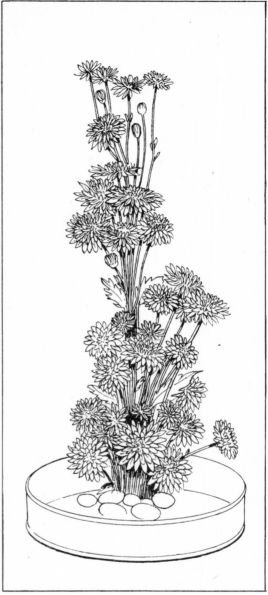

The ordinary becomes extraordinary

I have broken the rules! Crossing lines are only artistically permissible if they do something for an arrangement and when you feel thoroughly competent. The major fundamentals of proportion, balance, design, rhythm and repetition have by now been understood and learnt so that you can occasionally, for special reasons, break a rule to achieve originality and distinction.

Spray chrysanthemums are full of potential and reasonably priced but they are difficult to arrange for they are tall, stiff and quick to snap at you if you attempt the slightest liberty. Here is one of my answers.

Walking through the garden, I seized with joy this dried aloe candelabra to add to my treasure trove. I could have left it out of this arrangement. The line drawing indicates how it would have looked, an upright tiered design. This is very pleasing but a little ordinary. By building the vertical within the candelabra in this all-round arrangement and containing it in the round bowl, I have expressed a feeling of dual rhythm which makes the design jump out of the ordinary.

The tawny shades and tints of the flowers and dried aloe match perfectly and although it would appear that I could have done without the strong V-lines at the rear, the arrangement would then have been too flat. Had I removed them the circular effect and necessary depth would have been sadly missing as it was viewed from all sides.

Birds in a tizzy

The gay twirl of seaweed caught my leg while I was swimming. I turned the tables on my captor and it motivates this arrangement which is so throbbing with rhythm that words are superfluous to the visual message.

My perky strelitzia birds raise their crests in alarm at the seaweed snake winding its way round and under their iron pot in emulation of their strong horizontal beaks.

texture
and scale

Texture is a self-explanatory word which, in flower arranging, relates to fabrics and furnishings as well as to leaves, flowers and containers. It embraces weight, strength and general feel and is closely associated with scale.

Scale is the very important size relationship factor. There must always be a sense of smooth transition from one grade of size to another such as from one flower to its neighbour. A jerk in this transition of scale and texture can spoil what could otherwise have been a pleasing arrangement of flowers.

The container, too, must be selected for its size, colouring and for its textural and aesthetic suitability to the other materials in the whole arrangement or composition.

From the cradle, women, particularly, learn that certain things team-up successfully. They learn to relate the suitability of flower-trimmed hats with light summery dresses and this equates in the flower world with dainty silvery foliage or soft-looking greenery arranged with sweet peas, petunias or similar flowers.

Papyrus foliage, phormium and sansevieria could accompany strelitzias or clivia flowers in the same way as a well-tailored worsted suit and felt hat combine to make a smart but sturdy ensemble of distinction.

The bold arrangement of waratahs and prickly pears epitomises heavy texture. There is nothing soft and yielding about these components. The magnificent waratah is well matched and equally partnered by the tough prickly pear. As is so often the case with such materials, they are both very long-lasting. The pears survive for months, even without water, before showing any tiredness and the waratahs, too, last for many weeks. A well pinholder was used to hold the stems firmly and it was hidden from view by the separate piece of curving 'pear' which swings around the pinholder to conceal it.

The upright prickly pear posed the problem of how to fix this weighty and truculent fellow. First I dethorned him, handling him very gingerly I must add, and then I used the base of a heavy iron display stand to impale him very firmly. It also withstood his weight perfectly.

Waratahs have very heavy flower heads and so I used a contact cement to hold the well pinholder firm, levelling it with the aid of another pinholder as the illustration shows.

For a good example of a light-textured arrangement turn back to page 46 and look again at the very dainty blushing bride proteas held in their delicate shell container. Colouring, texture and size are all in unison with each other so there is nothing to jar one's sensibilities.

On page 48 you see a very marked contrast. The king protea, the largest and heaviest textured of this big family, is lording it on his own in a much sturdier container, accompanied by the suitable companions of heavy-textured sisal leaves and sansevieria.

In addition to considering their relative texture and size when selecting materials to use together, there is also their suitability with regard to the time, place and occasion of the arrangement. You have to choose those things which are in complete overall unity.

The container in the colour plate on page 71 is a French period urn in bronze which is suitable for a traditional type of medium-textured arrangement. Here it contains roses for an elegant social gathering with a length of gold lamé cloth draped to fashion a colour-linked base.

Cottage flowers could be arranged in a stout-looking ceramic jar with homespun tweed as the ideal material for the base. Like-to-like – got it?

A large and dressy occasion calls for a bigger demonstration with bold materials and most probably a more fulsome arrangement. A dinner party, on the other hand, needs something dainty, small and light weight in effect to be in keeping with your best china and crystal.

For a luncheon – business or social – the arrangement could be stronger, using heavier coarser materials, although it does not, necessarily, need to be bigger. Remember that you still have to see each other comfortably across the table and you must, also, leave adequate space for the food and condiments. How about

marigolds in a bold casserole dish – oven-
ware is made in such lovely rich colours –
or a well-blended mixture of bright dahlias
in a black container or a copper bowl?

You might be celebrating a sporting
occasion at home or doing the flower
arrangements for a party at the club house.
You could link the container, its type and
shape, with the particular event. For a
tennis success, how about using the
trophy itself for the centrepiece? The
inside should be carefully protected by a
piece of plastic sheeting and then either
filled with cellular brick or a pinholder and
wire netting could be used. Old whitened
tennis balls, which have had their tops cut
off rather like clean-cut breakfast eggs,
could be filled with cellular brick and
placed in position beside each lady guest.
A small piece of Florists' Bostik or Pres-
Stik will keep them from rolling and will
firmly attach them to the table, leaving no
tell-tale marks upon the polished surface
when the guests depart with their 'trophies'.
The whole scheme could be carried out in
medium-textured materials using flowers
in a colour scheme of green and white.

Another important consideration is
that of seasonal togetherness. One of the
secrets of the Japanese arranger is that he
groups together branches, shrubs, foliage
and flowers which are seasonal companions, that is those found growing together at the same time and sharing the
same habitat.

Spring fever

During the spring months, do you often
come home with a bunch of flowers, tulips
and iris perhaps, and wonder how best to
make them look impressive? Their comparatively short stems, caused by early
forced growth, do not allow much scope
for ingenuity when they are arranged on
their own. However, if you introduce a
dormant branch from the orchard, the
flowers will immediately gain in stature.

Medium-textured flowers should be
combined with a medium-textured branch
and as tulips are often grown under fruit
trees in an orchard, early varieties flowering before the trees blossom, the branch
in this arrangement strikes just the right
note. To make the composition still more
natural, I have contained it in a muted-
coloured ceramic dish, which is slightly
raised on shallow feet and has an attrac-
tively turned rim. A few stones conceal
the pinholder and finish the arrangement.

Down the drain

Seasonal togetherness is very well expressed in this picture. In fact, all the points which I have been stressing in this chapter are contained in this one arrangement.

The texture of the heavy red gum branch, with its woody seed pods and few sturdy leaves, is a perfect companion for the two enormous Japanese chrysanthemums in their ponderous, stout-hearted container. This antique-looking vase has been highly admired although it is only, in fact, a cast-iron water drain which I discovered on a scrap heap. Vigorous cleaning with a wire brush was more than rewarded and it has an ordinary tin as a water-holding liner.

Note the scale relationship between the flowers, branches and container. The season is shared and expressed by the autumn-into-winter branches and the traditionally winter-flowering chrysanthemums.

These show-specimen, pot-grown chrysanthemums can seldom be used successfully because they are so massive yet year after year you see them being proudly borne home by purchasers on the last day of flower shows. I always stand and wonder whether they will be really as pleased with them at home. These flowers are very difficult to arrange and they require the right material to accompany them. Seldom use more than two in an arrangement.

This variety of eucalyptus tree does not grow in the temperate climates but a good substitute can be found in many other trees. Select the heaviest branches and trim them to a good line. A gnarled oak, cut, trimmed and partially defoliated and then placed in a glycerine and water solution for a fortnight or so, is one suggestion. Keep some of the leaves in clusters as shown here. I have left fewer leaves than I would with oak because the heavy showy seed pods of the gum do not need much moral support.

Sea shore

Here is a happy and unusual way of making five flowers go a long way and it is eminently suitable for a smorgasbrod buffet. The composition is made up of many parts but the common denominator is water. Irises, as a family, are not averse to damp conditions and the twirly piece of seaweed, incorporating the rhythm of the sea, just asked for the inclusion of sponges, starfish and shells. And so we have materials with the same background and a liking for the same conditions.

In texture, too, they are alike. The seaweed looks heavy in the picture but it is, in fact, very light. The size transition is well graduated. The seaweed is the instigator of the design with the large sponge to the back and the three smaller pieces of a different species fanning out in front. The iris blooms gradually step down in size with no jumps from one extreme to another and the shells and charming little starfish complete the design.

Three-dimensional

This is the all-important dimension of depth. Most newcomers to the art of arrangement experience difficulty with regard to this and in consequence end up with flat designs which are all on one plane. This fault is passable if the arrangement is viewed only from a direct frontal approach but it is very ugly in a semimass design and impossible in a real mass because a one plane working allows too little room for the sufficiency of materials needed. The arrangement would overflow and bulge in a very ugly manner in the front making it unbalanced both visually and physically.

Recessing

is the answer

All arrangements depend for effect upon light and shade and this is achieved by recessing, an action with the flowers and foliage somewhat like that of an organist using the stops for depth and strength of tone.

Dark-coloured big flowers and/or foliage can be set in deep at the centre of an arrangement with lighter-coloured and smaller ones flowing out and upwards.

In mass designs, especially, although it is necessary to all, provision is made for this by commencing a design to form an embracing curve clearly shown in this facing construction picture which looks down on the first main lines of an arrangement in position.

The finished arrangement is a design without foliage and is a moderately massed fan shape. Dark pink roses are set in at the centre with spray chrysanthemums, in paler tints of pink, and delicate stems of Queen Anne's Lace, from the hedgerows, radiating outwards. This arrangement depends for its effect upon the strong contour and the number of flowers which although massed are nevertheless not too crowded.

The softening touch
of pine

Traditionally pine is used in Japan to symbolise joyfulness and I love it for its easy availability, tangy refreshing scent and last, but certainly not least, its pliable stems.

Within reason one can shape pine stems to comply with a design and I have coaxed the natural curve into the exaggerated swirls to introduce into this arrangement

the softening touch that these stiff and haughty chrysanthemums require to show them off to their best advantage.

The delicacy of the pine needles corresponds with the individual petals of the bold incurving flowers while both branches and flowers in their entirety conform to a medium-heavy textured arrangement of subtle distinction.

A pinholder holds the stems firmly impaled beneath the concealing aralia leaf – its cousin fatsia would be even more attractive – the indentations breaking up what might otherwise appear to be too solid a mass for the other components in this arrangement.

Employ voids

By copying the ancient Greeks and the artistic Japanese arrangers, we learn to employ voids in line designs. A trilinear plane is formed by stressing outlines and emphasising distance, middle distance and foreground. This is demonstrated in this arrangement of three stark white chrysanthemums and three cycas palm leaves held on a pinholder within a beautiful austere, muted black ceramic bowl with matching triangular base.

Judicious trimming of the palm foliage has resulted in greater definition of form which is accentuated by all the stems of the arrangement swinging up together as if growing in unison. The all-important, three dimensional depth is carefully preserved by the slight backward swing of the tallest, and incidentally the least mature, flower followed by the middle stem tilted slightly off-centre. The most mature flower is the lowest in this simple, uncluttered line design. In the accompanying bird's eye view, photographed from directly above, you can see the trilinear demarcation exactly as is, with nothing added or subtracted, except from the middle flower which had to be moved an iota from the true position to allow the central upright palm to be seen from this angle.

The completed design is a perfect example of the cantilever construction of asymmetrical balance. The density of the two main components, the short left-hand palm and one flower close to the central plumb line, balance a single unit, the long palm swinging exaggeratedly to the right. The flower dead on the centre line and the top flower slightly 'weighted to the right counterbalance to some extent the centre palm which is veering to the left.

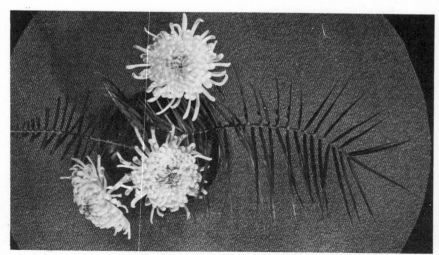

colour
harmony

In the previous chapters you have been discovering the power and necessity of line and learning how to achieve it. It is now time to turn our attention to an understanding and appreciation of colour and the impact it has on line and design.

Flowers and colour are synonymous. I have yet to see a grey flower and I do not want to. If flowers had scent but no colour, would they give us anything like the joy we have in them? Of course not. It is the combination of form, colour, and scent that makes a God-given flower.

Colour has a terrific impact on all of us throughout our daily living all our lives and by understanding we can use it to advantage. Pity the unfortunate small minority who are completely colour blind and who live amidst a mixture of greys.

Colours are the visible wavelengths of radiant energy. When a beam of sunlight is projected on to a white or neutral surface through a prism, seven beautiful colours or hues, to be correct, of the solar spectrum can be seen. These are violet, indigo, blue, green, yellow, orange and red, the colours of the rainbow.

The primary sunlight colours are orange-red, green and violet-blue. The secondaries are mixtures of the more obvious primaries. In our manufactured colour, the reverse is true. Pigment primaries are green-blue, yellow and magenta-red and these are combined to produce colour value.

Shades are pure hues deepened by the addition of black. Tints are produced by mixing in white and a tone is the result of adding grey – an admixture of black and white.

Colour evokes an emotional response according to the personality of the viewer. It has psychological and physical effect.

Ebullient people are visually soothed and quieted by the calming influence of the receding colours – blues, greens and mauves – towards which they find themselves automatically drawn. More introverted personalities prefer the stimulating, advancing hues which are, of course, the reds, yellows and oranges.

The advancing colours, especially the pure hues and their shades, absorb and retain sunheat, acting as radiators or conductors. They, therefore, work literally, and also through our sight appreciation, to raise temperature. Alternatively the receding hues are noticeably colder. Their shades, because of the depth of black within them, do absorb heat but not with the same effect as those of the advancing triplet.

The tints of the entire spectrum deflect and reflect the sunlight. Those of the advancing trio are especially cheering and the pale pink known as peach, which is derived from orange-red, is rated one of the most popular colours especially among women who instinctively, it would seem, prefer to be cheered whereas men prefer shades and strangely those of the receding colder colours especially blue. I am convinced that the strong sex are born with centrally heated circulation! So many men scorn modern heating aids. Certainly I do not require an electric blanket while I am blessed with my most efficient human hot-water bottle.

As I have already stated, colour influences us both physically and psychologically. Dual nerves in our eyes accept one hot and one cold colour simultaneously. These paired hues are blue and orange; red and green – opposites or mates of the spectrum. You will readily see this if you paint or visualise a rainbow and fashion it into a circle.

These mates or complementaries give an after-image. If you look at red the colour is intensified because the after-image projects a carry-over of green. This also happens with blue and orange. Test yourself for the after-image by staring intently at something red for a few seconds and then switch immediately and directly to a neutral (light) surface and you will see the identical shape in green and vice versa.

Interior decoration

As fleetingly mentioned while discussing colour balance on page 34, there are three main colour combinations much used and liked.

Complementary colour schemes are marriages of opposites which are, of necessity, one hot and one cold colour. They pack a terrific punch because of their physical effect upon us.

Analogous colour schemes consist of short sequences of neighbouring hues limited to two, or at the most, three. For example, orange and yellow which results in a warm arrangement or mauve, blue and green for a cooling effect.

Monotone schemes, as one would expect, are of one colour. They can be very charming if full advantage is taken of all the tints, tones and shades. They can be advancing or receding but obviously not both.

Since the main living rooms of our homes cannot be completely geared to one person's temperament and reaction, although the taste and requirements of the housewife usually and correctly dominate, the solution is a compromise of both hot and cold hues introducing some shades and a lot of tints. Select the colouring to suit the purpose of the room and its aspect and spice it with your own good taste and by original and beautiful flower arrangements. The aspect of the room is most important.

Cold rooms, especially those in cool climates that do not get much or any direct sun, definitely require a preponderance of advancing colours and depths of shade. Select your carpets and furnishings from the variety of gorgeous rich colourings offered in the orange-red, tawny-orange, mustard-gold ranges interspersing strong touches of a complementary hue, if some contrast is desired, according to your taste. Alternatively a monotone scheme in shades and tints can be very lovely and relaxing, brightened with a splash of rich colouring in a well-designed flower arrangement which is also in a monotone scheme but of a contrasting hue.

For sunny rooms, especially those in warmer climes, the receding hues come into their own and you would be wise to let tones and tints dominate. Flowers in such a setting could be in cool monotones in receding colours including green, white or a combination of the two, or with an expanse of water, as the fountain and pool arrangement on page 62.

Make sure that anyone calling at your home carries away a good impression. After considering colour and its effect upon yourself and others, try putting the theories into practice within your own decorative schemes and with regard to any changes contemplated in the furnishings. The purpose of this chapter is to help you discover that flowers, which are selected with knowledge, arranged with skill and sited correctly for both everyday living or a special occasion, will combine to unify the harmony of your home.

The hall is the first and last room seen by your visitors. They may not be apparently conscious or knowledgeable about flowers but they will be affected by the colour and form of their surroundings as any psychologist will bear out.

If your hall is small and on the dark side, a monotone scheme of decoration with a red-carpeted floor, pale peach-pink walls and plain or strictly self-patterned curtains will convey an impression of light and space.

Patterns require more accommodation for they tend to dwarf a room. In a sitting room, floral patterns in the upholstery and curtains could vie with each other and with the flowers unless you are clever enough to unify the flowers and patterned furnishings.

If sunlight bathes your entrance hall, use receding hues. Mingle a tone of citron (betwixt green and yellow) with tints and shades of olive or leaf green and again promote a sense of spaciousness by exercising restraint with regard to patterns.

Create bold arrangements for your hall and let them radiate a joyful welcome.

The study or small retreat can be a hallowed spot and it is more used than you would imagine when you stop to think about it. It is where the man of the house relaxes and where his wife takes her knitting or writing to be with him. Friends may pop in there to use the telephone or browse among your books and it deserves a flower arrangement. The colour illustrations of the next five arrangements are on pages 78 and 79.

Warm and cool

The graceful, horizontal sweeping form of this arrangement, designed for a study, is soothing but not too relaxing. We are supposed to be working, albeit unhurriedly. This analogous colouring incorporates two advancing and one receding hue. The calming green of the chianti bottle is enlivened by the orange tulips and yellow carnations to keep us awake.

The beautiful lazy line, best viewed from beneath, lends itself particularly well to a room requiring all its available elbow space. Here it sits high and out of the way and, with like-to-like in mind, it is placed among the aristocrats of my books, leather-bound classics.

A candlecup holder was fitted into the neck of the bottle and this contained a block of cellular brick held on a special holder – a flat piece of lead fitted with holding spikes rather like a carving dish. It is easier to achieve gentle horizontal curves when plastic brick is used.

Horizontal designs are ideal for bedrooms and sickrooms for when executed in tranquil mauves, greens or blues and placed on a dressing table or bedside table, they are generally seen from below by someone either seated or in a reclining position who will be able to enjoy to the full their sense of quiet rhythmic peace combined with quiet colouring to induce sleep.

Action stations

Activity is the keynote for living rooms. Arrangements call for a judicious mixture of stimulation and relaxation. They should incorporate hot and cold hues with one or the other predominating according to the aspect of the room.

The lovely Louis mirror in the previous colour plate reflects a pleasant cool-aspect room furnished primarily in gold which, along with gilt, is basically yellow in hue. A soft old-gold carpet teams with plain paler gold curtains and lampshades while purple-blue velvet upholstery and flowers contribute the complementary accent.

Upon a gold inlaid marquetry bureau, I have arranged twin designs in a pair of typical French period vases. *Longifolium* lilies keep company with the French atmosphere and purple campanulas introduce the complementary contrast of colour in this tightly packed paired design.

Dinner is served

Entertaining a number of people is made easier when you decide upon a buffet meal and success will be yours if you plan the food with colour knowledge because we eat food with three of our senses – sight, smell, and, of course, taste.

Choose a colour scheme according to whether the meal is supper or lunch. Night time is cooler and because of this and the abundance of bright hues displayed in colourful salads, jellies and mixed fruits, the flower arrangement designed for this meal needs to be substantial and colourful enough to hold its own but not to struggle with the goodies for attention. Polychromatic colour harmony – looking as jolly as it sounds, a scintillating medley of mixed hues – is what I have selected to enhance the spirit of the evening, the spirit itself being represented by the liqueur incorporated into the design. This colour scheme cannot often be used successfully. It usually needs an occasion like this but at the right time and in the right place it can look marvellous.

As the expert coachman controls his high-spirited horses with reins, so you must control the colour power in this type of harmony. Five 'reins' of colour flow from the focal point where the fruit and flowers merge. Yellow and blue irises swing up from the yellow bananas to divide into two streams of colour; one in blue and the other in yellow.

Orange tulips break into another dual stream. The upper merges into the peach tints of the gladioli, the lower merging into the orange-red chrysanthemums which bring the eye back along the length of the bottle into the rich colouring of the fruit, terminating in the fifth colour of the green grapes. Incidentally it is worth mentioning in passing that after the guests eat their way through the fruit course, this arrangement remains unspoiled – a feature to aim at in such designs.

Mix'n'match

Patterned upholstery and curtaining – a subject I have broached upon earlier – is one of the chief obstacles to an effective floral decor but both can be reconciled in an arrangement which can result in originality.

After dinner the ladies usually beat a retreat to the quiet domain of the bedroom so how about arresting their attention with a distinctive arrangement.

Our bedroom is circular with a sweeping curved headboard following the curving wall to form continuous bedside shelves allowing ample space for books, lamp and those important flowers.

In the tradition of bedroom decor, the inevitable floral curtains tempted me. The traditional floral design with its neutral background matches the neutral carpet and amalgamates with the neutral-tinted walls. Had the walls been painted in a contrasting colour, the curtains would jump at you instead of becoming an aesthetically pleasing part of a harmonious whole. By happy inspiration I continued the floral theme with a bedspread of identical material and this immediately strikes a very congenial and unifying note especially as the windows, which overlook the sea, curve round half the room and the curtains are florally balanced within the room by the matching bedspread.

The secret of success when matching flower arrangements with floral patterned furbishings is to identify as closely as possible with the textile prototype of flowers. This is easy when your chintz portrays flowers clearly but when the textile artist allows imagination to run riot over nature it is more difficult.

I chose roses and carnations to portray the type and as turquoise is not found in natural foliage I by-passed that difficulty with an unusual monotone colour scheme in magenta-red to match the predominant flower colour in the furbishings.

Lady of the bath

In the bathroom we are kept company by a graceful figure, reminiscent of an Egyptian bather as she picks her way daintily through swaying papyrus and cyperus reed to refill her waterpot at the bath tap.

The delicately coloured tiles and the burnt amber towel and tap knobs, the violet-pink of the anthuriums and the graceful billbergia with pale green and magenta flower scapes combine with the green foliage to produce this triad scheme in tints and shades of three colours – magenta, green, and orange. Triads are not really outstanding colour schemes and it is the design based on the graceful accessory rather than the colour scheme which renders this arrangement so attractive.

Going back downstairs, our attention is arrested by a blaze of colour. At the turn of the passage, where it widens sufficiently to accommodate a small chest of drawers, we see a self arrangement of glowing red tulips in a green dolphin-shaped vase. The narrow tailored design in a lovely complementary colour scheme suits this position well. The design of the container is continued in the vertical arrangement of the tulips and the soft green of the gracefully folded tulip leaves follow the sculptured curve of the bowl.

People are not brave enough about their colour schemes. Too often one finds a room decorated in only tints of equal value with no shades or deeper tones to give depth, strength and vitality. Treated in this timid way, a complementary scheme fails because it looks quite anaemic but this passage has a rich red carpet and soft nile green walls. The curtains are apple green. These colours combine to make a successful complementary scheme wherein one colour enhances the other through the after-image which the tulip arrangement endorses. Pale pink flowers with or without foliage would look lovely in this same setting because peach pink is a tint of red. You could also ring the changes with an all-green arrangement or introduce an analogous touch by using an appropriately coloured container such as this narrow cylindrical brass shell case.

Useful

and beautiful relics

This relic from 1917 makes an excellent container. It is heavy so there is little chance of it being knocked over, and sleek with no protrusions to catch the passer. The design of pink lilies and dark green foliage is trimly tailored to take up little space in a narrow hall or passage. It would be eminently suited to an odd ledge perhaps by a staircase where there is much coming and going.

With the introduction of yellow via the brass container, the colour scheme is no longer complementary but analogous green and yellow with complementary pink.

On the shelf

Many houses possess a somewhat restricted area at the approach to or at the top of the stairs or adjacent to the front door yet these make good strategic positions for flower arrangements. Here is a shellful of summer roses designed for such a position. It has been placed on a narrow marble shelf which hangs beneath a matching mirror. The proportions of this arrangement are arrived at horizontally in order to leave the mirror unobstructed.

The dainty scallop shell repeats the rhythm of the Italian scroll work in the marble while the rich yellow and amber colouring of the roses harmonises monochromatically with the gilt and amber flecks in the otherwise neutral-coloured marble. Some choice pieces of rose foliage, which are deep bronze, continue the monotone scheme assisted by the neutral colour of the shell.

Home brew

Once again the brass shell comes into its own. The five gladioli are so arranged to make the most use of the natural curves and this whole design would rise clear of the clutter of bottles and glasses at a party. The main stem, which is in tight bud, sets the line with a right to left swerve accentuated by the pronounced asymmetrical swing of the gladiolus on the extreme right. This outward-flowing gladiolus is balanced by the old-timer pistols which substitute for a base and co-operate with the flowers in a good design to promote a bar-like atmosphere.

Highly polished brass and natural golden-hued wood combine to heighten the general impression and the pale greeny-yellow gladioli, along with their own dark green foliage, and creamy pampas grass provide another striking example of an analogous colour scheme of brass, brassy-yellow and green.

Tête-à-tête

The fireplace is so often the sinecure of all eyes. How appropriate then to incorporate into this hub of household warmth the cheering note of beautiful flowers unusually and artistically arranged. This fireplace lends itself to floral exploitation for it has an extended mantelshelf and raised hearth. This two part arrangement in twin containers and a complementary colour scheme provides visual warmth to accompany the cosy comfort of leaping flames. The flowers are chrysanthemums in rich tawny-red shades with blue-green foliage selected for its height, availability and ability to be fashioned into the desired curves by gentle hand pressure.

The upper arrangement could stand on its own strength, complete in itself. It is asymmetrically balanced. The curved back tucks into the corner and the arrangement swings out towards the fire and the rest of the room. A strong downward subsidiary sweep extends below the container to link with the arrangement beneath.

The lower arrangement could also stand on its own merits if the foliage swinging left and up to meet the downward sweep of the upper arrangement was cut away to leave only the strong diagonally biased upright which echoes the diagonal line of the chimney stack.

Together, with one leading into the other, they make a fulsome and eye-arresting composition and the carved animal and human figures complete the integration of the two units into one whole. Notice that the main stem of the upper arrangement is kept to normal proportions but that the rim of the urn is concealed by the low placement of the focal chrysanthemum and the continued downward sweep of the lowest flower and foliage. This is the correct way to treat an arrangement which is placed fairly high and viewed from beneath as one reclines in an easy chair.

Conversely, arrangements at floor level or a foot or so above are seen from above and normal proportionate cutting of the main stem would look ridiculously short. A standing adult looks monstrously tall to a small child and the child appears very short to the adult looking down. In like manner the viewing height of an arrangement must be considered and the stems cut to the corresponding correct proportions. The higher the placement, the less height but more 'knee coverage' is necessary or 'skirt' as I often express it. Accentuated height and no 'skirt' is correct for an arrangement well below eye level.

Fireside niche

These lilies and the driftwood beside a stone fireplace provide a good example of a low placement arrangement. Proving the exception to the rule this has turned its back on the fire because it is a corner fireplace and the asymmetrical movement leads the eye into the room. The height is not as exaggerated as in the lower one of the pair we have just been considering. This is because it stands higher, some two feet above floor level and it is not an upright arrangement for the driftwood is a good twice the width of the wooden base. The rhythm in this design is in sympathy with the curving copper bowl behind it and would therefore be kept much lower if placed at the more usual table height.

Lasting impressions

This arrangement for a hall – a crescent-shaped design, executed in mauvey-pink gladioli, belladonna lilies and dahlias – points or directs one to the stairs and down the passage and also follows the rhythmically circular movement of the convex wall mirror. A Persian rug in softly muted tones reflects the soft analogous colour harmony of violet, violet-red and green while the soft lilac-pink walls enhance the rich warmth of the magenta (violet-red) stair carpet. Magenta, with its tints, is generally liked by both sexes and it is recognised as the hue to promote a sense of harmony and goodwill to envelop your guests on arrival and departure.

instant arranging

In general, arranging flowers is a leisurely, pleasurable occupation with a therapeutic effect. However, as we live in times that call for speed, it is sometimes necessary to take some short cuts and in doing so we must also learn to practise economy. I decided that I would devote this chapter to extending the modern craze for 'instant this' and 'instant that' to instant arranging.

I am always stressing the importance of the maxim that the success of an arrangement depends on what you leave out rather than what you put in. This is demonstrated throughout this chapter wherein one or two flowers replace the many and in some cases are left out altogether.

Using up the left-overs from other arrangements is an amusing challenge. Your knowledge and ability to do this in turn enables you to discipline yourself to leave out the extra material which is nearly always the undoing of an otherwise lovely design.

Whether you are browsing in a junk shop, attending a bazaar, bidding at an auction or just rummaging through the attic, you should always be on the alert for containers and accessories which will contribute beauty and originality to your arrangements.

The stereotype or mass-produced bowl or vase can belong to anyone's collection and with it you will be hard pressed to create an original arrangement. However, some cast-off oddity can trigger off a unique design which will cause many a favourable comment. I am lucky enough to possess the outdated laboratory gadget used in the colour illustration on page 67 and again in this chapter and also the chemical measure spoiled for photographic purposes by acetic acid which provided me with an original container possessing an unusual opaque effect (page 94).

At the other end of the scale can be found old china treasures such as a Victorian slipper or a figurine, like the one used in the arrangement on page 20, which may have a suitable hollowed portion, for example a basket, which can be used as the actual flower container.

Souvenirs from family holidays abroad can become highly individual flower holders in the hands of a resourceful arranger.

Nature's naturals

Sticks and stones can make the bones (to misquote the saying) of instant and contemporary arranging. Sticks fashioned by nature are very original, much more so than by man's imagination and carving, and they are there for us to discover or for them to discover us, occasionally somewhat painfully.

While swimming or paddling in warm seas, we are often accosted by seaweed which can be turned to good use (pages 65 and 73). Coral, too, is for the finding or, in temperate parts of the world, it can be bought from the more enterprising florists and, since each piece is seldom like any other, straight away you have a headstart on originality.

Strolling through the woods, I have come across lovely vines and ivies with weird and wonderful shapes which spell magic to me and make my fingers itch to get to work – stripping, cleaning, bleaching – grooming and preparing them for their important starring rôle in floral design.

Jumping Jack

Twin volcanic rocks team with a dried embryo cycas palm to create a torrid atmosphere for a couple of dried stems of kangaroo-paw plant which erupt from between the stones. The plant is so named because the edges of the flower sepals resemble the paws of this phenomenal jumper.

Confined within the spiral of a piece of bleached ivy, the design is arrestingly simple, quick and easy. It can be created with many combinations of differing stones and plants to ring the changes. Tall iris foliage and rushes with water-washed stones would also suit the design admirably and they would be as long-lasting and as quick to assemble as the example shown.

Painful finds

Stubbing your foot against a stone can be a painful but profitable experience. While chasing a cat from a choice clump of blue nepeta or cat's mint as it is appropriately, commonly called because all cats love its smell and soft, cushioning qualities, the rugged stone, sketched here, and my toe met each other! It has, however, proved its value as an important constituent of many an arrangement long after my toe stopped throbbing. I call it the Rock of Gibralter because of its silhouette resemblance to that promontory as viewed when approached by sea. It is the perfect accompaniment to any dried materials depicting arid conditions – like to like, remember!

Below is another arrangement of dried materials using montbretia foliage. These respond to this imaginative treatment which satisfies all artistic design requirements by the repetitive emergence of the leaves from the focal fir cone.

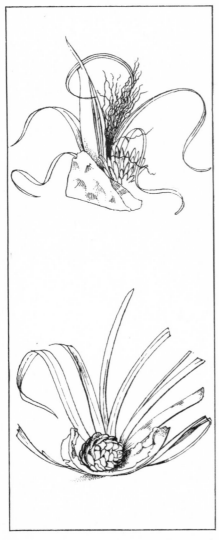

Follow my leader

This piece of driftwood, although quite ordinary in itself, strikes just the right line for the other components to follow. The acute angle was struck before it was finally nailed to the flat square of wood. Pieces of slasto (stone), left-overs from a job around the house, weight the wood and effectively conceal a small pinholder. The two small dried nutan proteas are also left-overs from a previous purchase of fresh proteas and here they have joined forces with a pine cone which is still attached to its branch.

The similarity between the dried foliage of the pine and protea and the shuttlecock shape of both the cone and flowers make this waterless permanent an outstanding arrangement. You can keep dried arrangements for many years, storing them in a cupboard for a season or re-assembling them differently when you grow tired of them. They can also be adapted to include a fresh flower or two which can be contained within a concealed water holder.

Barking up

the right tree

Some trees have the most fascinating and attractive bark. Examples include plane, birch, members of the pine family as well as those of the palm and gum tribe which are used here.

Long-lasting evergreen foliage or, better still, preserved foliage, as shown here, can provide a backdrop for a flower or two in season like the Christmas poinsettias introduced into this interesting line design which was formulated by curled aspidistra leaves emerging from a roll of bark. The leaves and flowers are contained in a small vessel of water hidden within the roll and they arise from the sandwiching curl. The flowers will last some time and the leaves will go on indefinitely to partner different flowers, succulents or whatever comes to hand.

If the leaves are preserved (page 13) and you wish to combine them with dry materials then the water can and should be omitted because although preserved foliage is indifferent to wet or dry conditions, dried materials must remain dry.

Self-contained

The busy arranger will no doubt appreciate other time-saving ideas which do not rely too heavily on dried and preserved material. Here is an arrangement comprised of only one stem of wisteria, selected for its enchanting self-contained pattern of twists which repeat, within its rhythmic swing, the movement of the container. All the unnecessary growth was selectively trimmed away and only the bottom twirl remains untouched.

It was arranged as unexpected guests were shown in at the front door although I must confess that I had spotted the possibilities of the wisteria previously – more a case of the 'seeing eye' in the selection and cutting than skill in the arranging.

At home

This arrangement proves that it is possible to arrange a bunch of flowers, just as well as one or two, in a hurry.

Your friends are due at any minute and there has been no time to arrange those flowers. How often we are caught this way. Quickly grab those carnations and hold them arranged in your hand. Deeply insert them into any attractive bottle you have handy, like this favourite of mine. Looped leaves at the right repeat the handle of the wicker casing on this madeira bottle and balance the outriding flowers. An instant arrangement to greet your friends.

Evergreen

The swirling seaweed certainly makes this arrangement, together with the discarded laboratory gadget which is the container. Greenery is so refreshing and in warm weather when flowers wilt so quickly what better than something of unusual and appealing form that lasts a week to ten days despite adverse conditions. A green monstera and three bronze canna leaves cradle the green seed heads which comprise the all-concealing focal point in yet another instant arrangement.

Solitary confinement

Rather than squeeze this extra rose into another arrangement and spoil that design, I placed it, in all its beauty, into a spoiled chemical measure. It was held within a Y-holder, cut from a piece of willow split down for a third to form a Y, which fitted tightly across the mouth of the container. The arrangement took exactly three minutes to put together and only required topping up daily with water. The flower was renewed every two or three days until the evergreen foliage dropped its leaves. Preserved foliage will obviate the necessity for change apart from the flower which can vary according to the season to provide a new look.

Nature's vase

This piece of driftwood has obvious potential. It is strong and solid at the base and I was just able to scoop out a hollow at the division of the branches which is deep enough to hold a few stems in water.

This is another occasion when the odd wine glass with a broken stem comes into its own. The broken stem is inserted deep into the wood and the glass is cradled within the hollow and filled with cellular brick. There is room and moisture enough to keep the five flowers happy. A yellowing monstera leaf harmonises with the flame and yellow kniphofias (red-hot pokers) and they are all arranged to follow the line prescribed for them by the driftwood. Neither effort nor time are required to think out this design for nature has provided the blueprint.

V for victory

These chrysanthemums have seen better days as part of a large composition which they have outlived. The leaves have gone the way of the dismantled arrangement and so it was necessary to hide the bare stems behind the facade of evergreen leaves.

For the fun of it I have arranged them in a well pinholder in front of the V-shaped palm boot, another of nature's naturals. It has been photographed off-centre to indicate a fly-past to demonstrate my hope that you have enjoyed yourselves reading this book and that I have succeeded in what I set out to do, to present this captivating art clearly and concisely, so that you, through your own enjoyable efforts, will be victorious.

96